J.-F. LELIF

ET APRÈS LE 4 JUILLET-LA 9

D0882540

ICA

rue Royale,-encoignu

9, PRÈS LA RUE DU CANAL

Février 1800

FÊTES MOBILES				QUATRE-TEMPS	
SEPTUAGÉSIME	1er février.	PENTECÔTE	24 mai.	PRINTEMPS	25, 27 et 28 F
CENDRES	18 février.	TRINITÉ	31 mai.	ÉTÉ	27, 29 et 30 M
PAQUES	5 avril.	FÊTE-DIEU	4 juin.	AUTOMNE	16, 18 et 19 Se
ROGATIONS	11 mai.	Premier dimanche de		HIVER	16, 18 et 19 D
ASCENSION	14 mai.	l'Avent	29 novembre.		

AVRIL ♈

soleil entre au Taureau le 20.

le 1, à 5 h. 1 m. soir.
Beau.
le 9, à 4 h. 1 m. soir.
Beau.
le 16, à 7 h. 33 m. matin
Pluie et vent.
le 23, à 5 h. 44 m. matin.
Pluie.

MAI ♊

- Le soleil entre aux Gémeaux le 20.

P L. le 1, à 9 h. 50 m. matin.
Variable.
D. Q. le 9, à 0 h. 53 m. matin.
Beau.
N. L. le 15, à 3 h. 57 m. soir.
Variable.
P. Q. le 22, à 8 h. 59 m. soir.
Beau par nord, pluie par sud.
P. L. le 31 à 0 h. 27 m. matin.
Beau.

JUIN ♋

Le soleil entre au Cancer le

D. Q. le 7, à 6 h. 59 m. m
Pluie et vent.
N. L. le 14, à 0 h. 33 m. n
Beau.
P. Q. le 21, à 1 h. 42 m. s
Très-pluvieux.
P. L. le 29, à 0 h. 29 m. so
Très-pluvieux.

	AVRIL			MAI			JUIN	
Mercredi.	Hugues.	1	Vendredi.	Jacques Philippe.	1	Lundi.	Pamphile.	
Jeudi.	François de P.	2	Samedi.	Athanase.	2	Mardi.	Marcellin.	
Vendredi.	*Vendr.-St.* Richard.	3	Dim.	Inv. Sᵉ Croix.	3	Mercredi.	Clotilde.	
Samedi.	Isidore.	4	Lundi.	Monique.	4	Jeudi.	*Fête-Dieu.* O	
Dim.	PAQUES. Vincent.	5	Mardi.	Pie V, pape.	5	Vendredi.	Quirin.	
Lundi.	Célestin.	6	Mercredi.	Jean P.-L.	6	Samedi.	Boniface.	
Mardi.	Hégésippe.	7	Jeudi.	Stanislas.	7	Dim.	Norbert.	
Mercredi.	Dionis.	8	Vendredi.	Désiré.	8	Lundi.	Médard.	
Jeudi.	Marie Egypt.	9	Samedi.	Grégoire.	9	Mardi.	Félicien.	
Vendredi.	N.-D.-S.-D.	10	Dim.	Gordien.	10	Mercredi.	Marguerite.	
Samedi.	Léon, pape.	11	Lundi.	*Rogations.* Mamert.	11	Jeudi.	Oct. F.-Dieu. I	
Dim.	*Quasim.* Vict., mart.	12	Mardi.	Nérée.	12	Vendredi.	Jeanne.	
Lundi.	Herménégilde.	13	Mercredi.	Jean le Silencieux.	13	Samedi.	Antoine de P	
Mardi.	Tiburce.	14	Jeudi.	*Ascension.* Pacôme.	14	Dim.	Basile.	
Mercredi.	Anastasie.	15	Vendredi.	Isidore.	15	Lundi.	Modeste.	
Jeudi.	Turibe.	16	Samedi.	Ubalde.	16	Mardi.	François Rég	
Vendredi.	Anicet.	17	Dim.	Paschal.	17	Mercredi.	Avit.	
Samedi.	Parfait.	18	Lundi.	Honoré.	18	Jeudi.	Marine.	
Dim.	Timon.	19	Mardi.	Yves.	19	Vendredi.	Julien.	
Lundi.	P. Nolasque.	20	Mercredi.	Bernardin.	20	Samedi.	Silvère.	
Mardi.	Anselme.	21	Jeudi.	Hospice.	21	Dim.	Aloise.	
Mercredi.	Soter.	22	Vendredi.	Julie.	22	Lundi.	Paulin de Nol	
Jeudi.	Georges.	23	Samedi.	*Vigile-J.* Didier.	23	Mardi.	Audry.	
Vendredi.	Fidelise.	24	Dim.	PENTEC. Vinc. de Lér.	24	Mercredi.	Nat. s. Jean-B	
Samedi.	Marc.	25	Lundi.	Donatien.	25	Jeudi.	Prosper.	
Dim.	Clet et Marcel.	26	Mardi.	Philippe Nér.	26	Vendredi.	Jean et Paul.	
Lundi.	Frédéric.	27	Mercredi.	*IV Temps.* Jules.	27	Samedi.	Crescent.	
Mardi.	Vital.	28	Jeudi.	Germain.	28	Dim.	Irénée.	
Mercredi.	Pierre, martyr.	29	Vendredi.	Maximin.	29	Lundi.	Pierre et sain	
Jeudi.	Catherine de Sienne.	30	Samedi.	Félix, m.	30	Mardi.	Comm. de s.	
		31	Dim.	*Trinité.* Pétronille.				

LEVER DU SOLEIL		Mois		COUCHER DU SOLEIL	

New Louisiana Gardener

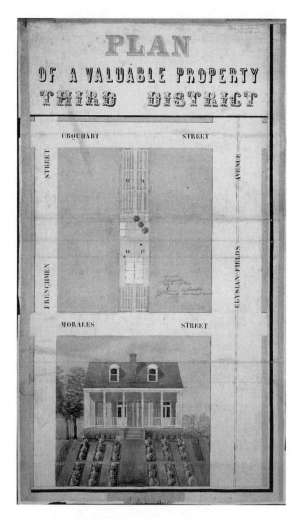

Garden laid out in rows and squares,
Faubourg New Marigny, 1858.
Courtesy of New Orleans Notarial Archives.

Jacques-Felix Lelièvre's

NEW LOUISIANA
GARDENER

Jacques-Felix Lelièvre

Translated, with an Introduction, by
SALLY KITTREDGE REEVES

Louisiana State University Press *Baton Rouge*

Copyright © 2001 by the Southern Garden History Society
All rights reserved
Manufactured in the United States of America
First printing
02   04   06   08   10   09   07   05   03   01
1   3   5   4   2

Designer: Barbara Neely Bourgoyne
Typeface: Cochin and Adobe Garamond
Typesetter: Coghill Composition, Inc.
Printer and binder: Thomson-Shore, Inc.

Published in cooperation with the Southern Garden History Society.

Library of Congress Cataloging-in-Publication Data

Lelièvre, J. F.
    [Nouveau jardinier de la Louisiane. English]
    Jacques-Felix Lelievre's New Louisiana gardener / translated, with an introduction,
by Sally Kittredge Reeves.
        p.   cm.
    Includes bibliographical references (p.).
    ISBN 0-8071-2479-6 (cloth : alk. paper)
    1. Gardening—Louisiana.   I. Title: New Louisiana gardener.   II. Title.
SB453.2.L8 L4613   2001
635′.09763—dc21   00-048556

The paper in this book meets the guidelines for permanence and durability
of the Committee on Production Guidelines for Book Longevity of the
Council on Library Resources. ♾

Dedicated to
SHINGO DAMERON MANARD

CONTENTS

FOREWORD

><+>+0+<+><

The Southern Garden History Society is pleased to have commissioned the English translation and publication of Jacques Felix Lelièvre's *Nouveau Jardinier de la Louisiane* along with an introductory essay to explain the significance of the little volume and its place in horticultural history. Written and published by Lelièvre in New Orleans in 1838, the *Nouveau Jardinier* is published here in an English translation for the first time.

The initial inspiration and strong continued support for this project came from Shingo Dameron Manard of Covington, Louisiana, a dedicated member of the Southern Garden History Society Board of Directors for many years. A well-worn original copy of the book is part of Mrs. Manard's library. Mrs. Manard credits her awareness and enthusiasm for the book to Samuel Wilson Jr., F.A.I.A., distinguished architect and noted historian of New Orleans who shared his copy of Lelièvre's book with her many years ago. She also involved the late Professor Joseph Ewan of the Missouri Botanical Garden, who wrote to her in 1995, "The history of Horticulture will profit enormously from your searches."

The Board of Directors and the Publications Committee of the Southern Garden History Society are indebted to Sally Reeves, Archivist, New Orleans Notarial Archives, for her translation of the book and for the many hours of research she devoted to reviewing primary source material in France and in the United States for her scholarly introduction to the text. By carefully researching Lelièvre's French background and literary sources as well as documents at the Missouri Botanical Garden and the New Orleans Notarial Archives, Sally Reeves has uncovered significant garden design and horticultural information that greatly influenced early- to mid-nineteenth century gardens in Louisiana and other areas where French settlement occurred. Dan Gill, Orleans Parish Horticulturist for the Louisiana State University Cooperative Extension Service, ably assisted with updating names of plants and horticultural terms.

The Southern Garden History Society wishes to thank Louisiana State University Press for recognizing the value of this project and supporting it with its talented staff and administration.

The Southern Garden History Society was formed in Winston-Salem, North Carolina, in May 1982, as an outgrowth of a continuing series of conferences on Restoring Southern Gardens and Landscapes held in Old Salem. The society's mission is to stimulate interest in southern garden and landscape history, in historical horticulture, and in the preservation and restoration of historic gardens and landscapes in the South. *Magnolia,* a quarterly publication of the society, is devoted to the gathering and dissemination of knowledge of southern garden history and reporting related events of interest to members. An annual meeting is held each spring in one of the southern states. Members represent all of the southern states from Texas to Maryland, the District of Columbia, many states outside the South, and a number of foreign countries.

WILLIAM C. WELCH
Southern Garden History Society President, 1996–1998
Publications Committee Chairman

FLORENCE GRIFFIN
Southern Garden History Society President, 1992–1994

ACKNOWLEDGMENTS

➤—┤◆➤—○—◀◆├—◄

Somehow I realized during the course of the luncheon to which Ethel Dameron (Shingo) Manard and Elizabeth (Betsy) Crusel invited me in early 1995 that the project they were suggesting on behalf of the Southern Garden History Society would have a profound impact on my life. To a lifelong gardener, Louisiana history enthusiast, and Francophile archivist, the opportunity to translate the long-obscure *Nouveau Jardinier de la Louisiane* for an audience of gardening connoisseurs was both challenging and invigorating. I knew even then that an uphill learning path awaited me. The members of the Society have made traveling that path a joy, and Jacques-Felix Lelièvre and the Society members have led me into new worlds of knowledge about both gardening and French horticultural history.

Shingo Manard, an extraordinary and generous civic leader of New Orleans, and author William C. Welch, Professor and Landscape Horticulturist at Texas A&M University, have been constant guides and confreres. To them the project owes its very being. They have advised, encouraged, corrected, and sustained me. They provided historical data, shared their files or publications, instructed me in gardening, and introduced me to other distinguished members of the Southern Garden History Society. Above all, their sense of the translation gave me needed direction when I would have made it too literal.

I am grateful to Betsy Crusel of New Orleans; Florence Griffin of Atlanta, horticulturist; Flora Ann Bynum of Old Salem, North Carolina, author of the *Old Salem Garden Guide;* Edgar Givhan of Montgomery, Alabama, physician, author, and garden designer; Peter Hatch, Director of Gardens at Monticello; Catherine Howett; Kenneth McFarland of Historic Stagville, North Carolina; Peggy Newcomb, Curator of Historic Plants at Monticello; and Ben G. Page Jr., Peter Quitmeyer, Edward Shull, and Jane Symmes, all of whom serve on the Board or the Publications Committee of the Southern Garden History Society. They provided information, gave acceptance and encouragement, made suggestions, and sometimes gave legal advice. Their suggestions for improving the introduction and the translation have been most welcome.

Wilbur Meneray, Head of Special Collections at Tulane University's Howard-Tilton Memorial Library, read the introduction in its early stages and made helpful suggestions. Special Collections includes the Manuscripts Department, where Lee Miller, Curator of Manuscripts, was helpful in providing access to the de Feriet Papers. There also I read the Caillé Lelièvre letters and Rozier's eighteenth-century French encyclopedia of natural history, which I am grateful that the late Jane Whitney purchased for Tulane. Gary Van Zante of Tulane's Southeast Architectural Archive was more than gracious, arranged for full copies of our working text, contributed bibliographical research, and gave access to the wonderful resources of the New Orleans Town Gardeners' Garden Library at the Southeast Architectural Archive.

Alfred Lemmon, Curator of Manuscripts at the Historic New Orleans Collection (HNOC), generously shared his contacts in Europe. Florence Jumonville, formerly with the HNOC and now Head of Special Collections at the University of New Orleans, showed me rare imprints at the HNOC, including Père Antoine's catechism, which Charles Jourdan published. Wayne Everard, ably assisted by Irene Wainwright, both of the Louisiana Division, New Orleans Public Library, made presentable the papers in the several lawsuits between booksellers Charles Jourdan and his onetime partner A. L. Boimare. Because of the care that Collin Hamer and his Louisiana Division staff have taken of various local district court records housed at the Library, researchers have access to succession records such as the cases that helped to shed light on the lives and careers of Lelièvre and his family. I thank the staff for these and other services, so cheerfully rendered.

Professor Joseph Ewan's pioneering work on the horticultural history of Louisiana, along with his insightful letters to Shingo Manard commenting on the *Nouveau Jardinier,* have been invaluable. Nesta Ewan of the Missouri Botanical Garden Library was both solicitous and helpful, as was Martha Riley, Archivist there. Dan Gill of the Louisiana Agricultural Extension Service most kindly read the translation and commented on its accuracy in relation to Louisiana's contemporary horticultural practices. Suzanne Turner of the Louisiana State University (LSU) School of Landscape Design read the introduction in its early stages, provided what proved to be critical research questions, and gave welcome encouragement. Her books and her lecture on Louisiana landscapes to the Louisiana Historical Society were instructive. I also thank Faye Phillips, Glenn McMullen, and other members of the staff of the Hill Memorial Library, LSU, which has the only copy of Ulger Vicknair's gardening guide I know of, and where we were able to view a copy of the *Nouveau Jardinier* that had been used in the Baton Rouge area.

Archivists in Europe were most generous in responding to mail requests. I especially thank Françoise Bermann of the Bibliothèque, Université de Caen, Basse Normandie, for research on Lelièvre's educational background and for sending me extensive notes on the histories both of horticulture in Caen and of the Botanical Garden there. I also thank Jean Saquet of the Université de Caen; Turbot Christophe, Webmaster of Caen; and Bruno Ricard, Centre des Archives de Nantes; and Monique Constant, Division historique, Direction des Archives, Ministère des Affaire Etrangères for their responses.

I am grateful to Buffie Hollis and Erin Heaton of the Notarial Archives, and to William M. Pratt, Custodian of Notarial Records of New

Orleans, for making images available. To my friend Maureen Detweiler I also owe gratitude for sharing with me her in-depth knowledge of antique roses. Finally, I wish to thank sincerely my husband and soul mate William D. Reeves for his generous assistance, deep understanding, and long-suffering interest in this project, and for having to move so many plants into new places in the garden as my fixation grew.

SALLY KITTREDGE REEVES

New Louisiana Gardener

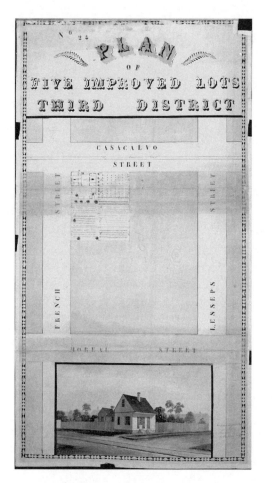

Market garden in Third District, 1866.
Courtesy of New Orleans Notarial Archives.

INTRODUCTION

❧━◆━○━◆━❧

I. Jacques-Felix Lelièvre

Louisiana historians generally agree that the French nation did a poor job of populating Louisiana during the eighteenth century when the colony was hers to build or lose.[1] Ironically, however, thousands of skilled Frenchmen fled Europe and the Caribbean in the wake of the French Revolution and its aftermath and found their way to New Orleans in search of a better life during the nineteenth century. There they built upon a surviving climate of sympathy to French culture, adding their own gifts to the city's life and economy. Their contributions to its art, architecture, and culinary arts are well known, as is their great influence on Louisiana law. They also made significant additions to the city's religious and educational institutions, as well as to its journalism, literature, theater, music, medical science, book-selling and publishing businesses, and even to its horticultural science. Owing in large part to their contributions, and despite significant competition from other ethnic groups, New Orleans for over a century after their arrival enjoyed a remarkably sophisticated and well-developed French culture. Indeed, elements of that culture survive to this day.

1. See, for example, Mathé Allain, *Not Worth a Straw: French Colonial Policy and the Early Years of Louisiana* (Lafayette, La.: Center for Louisiana Studies, University of Southwestern Louisiana, 1988); and Carl A. Brasseaux, *The Foreign French: Nineteenth-Century French Immigration to Louisiana* (Lafayette, La.: Center for Louisiana Studies, University of Southwestern Louisiana, 1990), 1:xi–xxx.

Jacques-Felix Lelièvre (1795–1854) was one of those nineteenth-century French nationals who left for the New World seeking greater prosperity and found it while enriching their adopted country. In an environment sympathetic to French culture, Lelièvre prospered as a bookseller, publisher, and occasional writer who specialized in providing publications and related materials for French-speaking Louisiana residents. Lelièvre spent twenty years in New Orleans in the prime of his life and at the height of the city's own fortunes, leaving to posterity the somewhat enigmatic present volume. Composed and published at his Royal Street shop and home in 1838 and printed by Gaux and Company at 108 Chartres Street, *Nouveau Jardinier de la Louisiane* is a slim volume of some two hundred pages of highly condensed prose. As the present translation reveals, the book reflects the author's cultural bias as well as his gardening knowledge. It demonstrates an impatience to improve the level of horticultural expertise in New Orleans by sharing the benefits of progressive French science. Lelièvre's *Nouveau Jardinier de la Louisiane,* although never reprinted until now, was the first and to this day is one of only two known French-language gardening manuals written in America.[2] Future scholars may wish to use this translation as they seek to measure Lelièvre's success, his true effect on Louisiana's nineteenth-century horticultural growth.

A native of Caen, a city of about 100,000 on the Orne River in Calvados, a small department of Normandy, Lelièvre was born in 1795 during the heat of the French Revolution. His mother, born Marie Henriette Jacqueline Perine Gervais, bore at least two sons and was herself a native of Caen. From his father, Nicolas Anne Lelièvre, a gardener

2. The other is Ulger Vicknair's *Le Jardinier Economique et Productif* (New Orleans, 1867), a handbook for vegetable growers in St. John the Baptist Parish, on the Mississippi River above New Orleans.

of Caen, Lelièvre probably learned gardening at an early age.[3] He must also have had formal schooling in horticulture at some point, for he represented himself on the *Nouveau Jardinier*'s title page as a "former gardener-horticulturist of the French Government for the colonies." Perhaps more significantly, he cited directly six of the most advanced botanical and horticultural works of the time in France and reflected their theory and practice in his own writing.

Lelièvre's acknowledged sources give us an idea of his educational background in horticulture. He cited first the seven-volume *Botanist Cultivateur*[4] of George Louis Marie Dumont de Courset, a Parisian botanist and follower of the pioneering "natural" classifying system of Antoine-Laurent de Jussieu. Dumont's popular treatise, first published in Paris in 1798, included instructions for the construction and layout of walls and beds in the orchard to protect and increase the product of fruit trees.[5] Lelièvre devoted a long chapter to this topic.

Lelièvre also noted *Le Cours de Culture* by André Thouin, a practicing horticulturist, correspondent of Thomas Jefferson, and longtime gardener-in-chief of the *Jardin du Roi* (King's Garden) in Paris.[6] Thouin had founded a school of practical agriculture at the garden, where he shared his research with students. The school's emphasis on acclimatiz-

3. *Extrait de registre des actes de decès de la Commune de Lauderon,* January 16, 1854, *No. 9 du registre decès,* in Succession of J. F. Lelièvre, 2DC 7441, Orleans Parish Courts (New Orleans Public Library, Microfilm VSB290/7398–7531).

4. The full title of this work is *Le Botaniste Cultivateur; ou Description, culture, et usages de la plus grande parties des plantes étrangères, naturalisées et indigènes, cultivées en France, en Autriche, en Italie, et en Angleterre, rangées suivant la méthode de Jussieu.* (Paris, 1798–).

5. Ad. Davy de Virville, *Histoire de la Botanique en France* (Paris, 1954), 92, 94, 98–99.

6. Today the garden of the Museum of Natural History on the Left Bank in Paris.

ing exotic plants brought back to the garden by French botanists who traveled all over the world to find and retrieve plants for the nation[7] would find its way into Lelièvre's writing. Thouin was also, and perhaps foremost, an expert on grafting, and he wrote extensively in the field. Again, Lelièvre reflected the influence with his emphasis on grafting, the *greffe.*

Thouin was also one of the authors of a twelve-volume agricultural and veterinary encyclopedia that Lelièvre cited. Entitled *Cours Complet d'Agriculture*[8] and published in Lyons toward the end of the eighteenth century, this series was edited by the Abbé François Rozier and included work by the agronomist and soil chemist Jean-Antoine-Claude Chaptal. Lelièvre also cited the agricultural scientists of the Institute of France, who at the turn of the nineteenth century had published *Nouveau Cours Complet d'Agriculture,*[9] a sixteen-volume "new and augmented" edition of the Rozier encyclopedia. This work contained long entries on soil types, grafting, pruning, digging, plant characteristics and pathology, botanical classification, insects, animal husbandry, meteorology, mineralogy, and a host of other topics that summarized contemporary science in natural history.

7. Marguerite Duval, *The King's Garden,* trans. Annette Tomarken and Claudine Cowen (Charlottesville: University Press of Virginia, 1982).

8. Abbé Rozier, ed., *Cours complet d'Agriculture théorique, practique, économique, et de médecine rurale et veterinaire: suivi d'une méthode pour étudier l'agriculture par principes: ou, Dictionnaire universel d'agriculture par un société d'agriculteurs, et redigé par M. L'Abbé Rozier,* 12 vols. (Paris and Lyons: Chez les Libraires associés, 1793–1805).

9. Institute de France, Section d'Agriculture, *Nouveau cours complet d'agriculture théorique et practique, contenant la grande et la petite culture, l'économie rurale et domestique, la médecine vétérinaire, etc.; ou Dictionnaire raisonnée et universel d'agriculture; ouvrage rédigé sur le plan de celui de feu l'abbé Rozier, duquel on a conservé les articles dont la bonté a été prouvée par l'expérience; par les membres de la Section d'agriculture de l'Institut de France, etc. Nouvelle ed., revue, corrigée et augmenteé* (Paris: Librairie Encyclopédique de Roret, [ca. 1821–23]).

Finally, Lelièvre used two single-volume manuals. He cited the first as *Le Manuel du Jardinier.* Lelièvre did not indicate the author, but it may have been the Parisian nurseryman Louis Noisette, whose 1826 four-volume *Manuel Complet du Jardinier, Maraîcher, Pépinièriste, Botaniste, Fleuriste, et Paysagiste*[10] had been condensed and published in a single volume in Brussels (1829). It is also possible that *Le Manuel du Jardinier* was a pirated edition of *Le Bon Jardinier,* explained below. The second manual Lelièvre described as *Le Jardinier Almanach,* literally "The Gardener Almanac," which was nevertheless almost certainly a single-volume annual horticultural encyclopedia entitled *Le Bon Jardinier.*[11] This hefty periodical first appeared in Paris in 1755 and had a series of editors and title variations over the years. It would provide not only ideas but also text for the *Nouveau Jardinier.*

Did Lelièvre find his way to Paris to absorb its effervescent ferment of botanical and horticultural research early in the nineteenth century? If so, he might have attended Thouin's lectures at the *Jardin du Roi* of the *Muséum National d'Histoire Naturelle.* There the botanical garden was a space devoted solely to the study of plants *en école* (as a school). The school was actually a garden where the growing plants were arranged according to a classification scheme—either that of Carl von Linnaeus or the competing scheme of Antoine-Laurent de Jussieu, a director of the garden. There the students gathered, as an 1803 publication described it, "books in hand, to study the plants, compare each to another, and learn as much as possible from observation or from the dissection of flowers and fruits."[12]

10. Paris, 1826.

11. *Le Bon Jardinier: Almanach Pour L'Année. . . .* The *Librairie agricole de la Maison Rustique* was the first publisher.

12. *Dictionnaire d'Histoire Naturelle, Appliqué aux Arts, Principalement à l'Agriculture et à l'économie rurale et domestique: Par une Société de Naturalistes et d'Agriculteurs,* Nouvelle ed. (Paris: Deterville, 1803), 12:259–60.

If Lelièvre did not study in Paris, the Caen of his youth was also an excellent place in which to develop an interest in scientific horticulture. The Botanical Garden of Caen was already 150 years old in his day, and with some 3500 plants and university management it was a center of both botanical study and civic pride for the Caennais. The University of Caen had offered a course in botany since 1438 in conjunction with its medical curriculum, the usual center of plant studies at that time. As early as 1509, scholars of Caen began publishing the results of plant-finding student excursions into the Norman countryside, and by the early nineteenth century, when Lelièvre was of school age, the garden's directors were publishing catalogs and guides that were important documents in the life of Caen.[13]

Lelièvre's eventual appointment as a horticultural specialist for the French colonial government suggests that he learned his science well. What severed him from this relationship with the French government is unknown. Perhaps it was a change of patronage following the July Monarchy of 1830; perhaps his own restlessness. In any case, at the end of 1833 he found himself in Rouen, not far from home, contemplating a move to America. To Jacques-Felix Lelièvre and to his brother Caillé Lelièvre, as to so many Frenchmen of their day, the United States was a beacon. It was, as Caillé wrote, a country "so beautiful, so verdant, [it is] the refuge of all who have nothing in their own land and to whom energy and industry promise a better sort."[14]

That remark, preserved in a letter that Caillé Lelièvre wrote to Jacques-Felix in the summer of 1835—some eleven months after the latter's arrival in New Orleans, sheds light on the general reasons for Jacques-Felix's removal to America. His emigration was part of a wide movement of Frenchmen from Europe to the United States at this time.

13. *"Le Jardin des Plantes D'Hier a Aujourd'hui," Liberté de Normandie* (Caen), 1976.
14. Caillé Lelièvre to Jacques-Felix Lelièvre, June 30, 1835, Caillé Lelièvre Letters, Tulane University Special Collections, MS B58.

As historian Carl A. Brasseaux has pointed out, economic dislocations originating with the French Revolution and Napoleonic wars, followed by economic distress in the French provinces during the 1820s and 1830s, sent thousands of Frenchmen to America during those decades. Poverty and famine were widespread in France among the working classes throughout the period. Agricultural stress, industrialization, political unrest, a financial panic in 1825, and a deep recession beginning in 1830 were among the factors that drained the population of France to the eventual gain of America. Lelièvre was one of at least twenty thousand Frenchmen who emigrated to Louisiana in the wake of the French Revolution.[15]

He sailed from Le Hâvre aboard the brig *Cazenave* and arrived in New Orleans on July 31, 1834. There was only one other passenger, perhaps because they were traveling during the off-season, or because the vessel had limited accommodations.[16] Lelièvre was not penniless, however. He brought a *mise de fonds* (financial stake) supplied by his brother, which he was expected to repay by a note "either of Paris or of Le Hâvre or Bordeaux."[17] Within roughly a year of his arrival in New Orleans, Lelièvre would value his assets at one thousand piastres (dollars).[18]

Jacques-Felix Lelièvre's first year in New Orleans was evidently tumultuous. The city was still reeling from the effects of back-to-back cholera epidemics that had nearly decimated its population during the

15. Brasseaux, *Foreign French,* 1:xiii–xx. This figure includes roughly ten thousand who arrived in 1809 and at least ten thousand who arrived by ship between 1820 and 1840. Brasseaux, in an abundance of caution, undercounted émigrés arriving by ship.

16. Work Projects Administration of Louisiana, Survey of Federal Archives in Louisiana, *Passenger Lists Taken from Manifests of the Customs Service in New Orleans,* 2 [1834–1838] (New Orleans, 1940), 17.

17. Caillé Lelièvre to Jacques-Felix Lelièvre, June 30, 1835, Caillé Lelièvre Letters.

18. Carlile Pollock, Notary Public [hereafter N.P.], June 23, 1835, New Orleans Notarial Archives [hereafter NONA].

previous two years. Lelièvre arrived in midsummer to face the sultry New Orleans climate in a season when relief from the heat could come only by way of ferocious thunderstorms that dumped torrents of rain onto mud-laden streets. If the newcomer welcomed evening when the heat abated slightly, he would still have to face the swarms of mosquitoes that emerged at sunset and buzzed about the ears. In the summer of 1834, New Orleans was still buzzing from the scandal of Madame Delphine Lalaurie, a wealthy matron whose maltreatment of her slaves had caused a riot to break out among the citizenry, three months before Lelièvre's arrival. Among the witnesses to these events was one "Fouché," possibly Xavier Fouché, Madame Lalaurie's neighbor and Lelièvre's future employer and brother-in-law.[19] Fouché could have related a firsthand account of the chilling tale to the newcomer.

Lelièvre's first letters to his brother back home were evidently tales of woe, perhaps combined with homesickness. On February 7, 1835, and again in March, he complained about the climate of Louisiana and the greed he saw in America, the indirect evidence for which survives in two of his brother's compassionate replies. Caillé Lelièvre's description of the promise of America quoted above was really an ironic response recounting what they had once believed about the New World's promise. Jacques-Felix's letters from New Orleans had in fact convinced Caillé to renounce their onetime dream of a life together in America. Instead, he and his wife had purchased a farm, L'Abadaire, in the *department* and *arrondissement* of Mayenne, two leagues from Beurloy. They planned to improve the land and believed they could recover a 10 percent return within a year or two. Jacques-Felix could join them if he wished. "If you do not succeed in this country and one day you want to return," Caillé wrote, "remember you always have us devoted to you. The house at L'Abadaire is spacious. There will be a place for us all."[20]

19. Henry C. Castellanos, *New Orleans as It Was: Episodes of Louisiana Life* (1895; reprint, Baton Rouge: Louisiana State University Press, 1978), 58–59.

20. Caillé Lelièvre to Jacques-Felix Lelièvre, June 30, 1835, Caillé Lelièvre Letters.

But Jacques-Felix Lelièvre did not give up on America. He could hardly have foreseen it, but better times lay just ahead of that cold, probably wet and penetrating February day when he wrote to his brother about the apparent uncertainty of his future. He had, in any case, already found work at a bookstore on Royal Street. Charles Jourdan, an elderly French bibliophile who had died two months before Lelièvre's arrival in New Orleans, had operated the store for decades on a prominent corner in the Vieux Carré. Eccentric, unpredictable, disorganized, eighty years old, and somewhat disoriented from a recent change of domicile, Charles Jourdan had left his book and stationer's store in disarray at the time of his death. The store abounded with thousands of unsorted volumes, some in prime condition, some barely salable. The shop was also filled with writing and drawing supplies, toys, and trinkets that Jourdan had been importing for decades from his native France. In the New Orleans Customhouse on Canal Street more trunks of children's toys and baubles lay waiting for the storekeeper.[21]

Jourdan's twenty-six-year-old nephew, Xavier Fouché, was working to impose some system upon the chaos while trying to settle the old man's estate. This was, to say the least, a difficult assignment. From Paris, Jourdan's estranged wife and married daughter were claiming debts still owed them from as much as twenty years earlier. There were legal claims in New Orleans; the old furniture and shopworn merchandise needed liquidating, and the disheveled shop needed organizing. Fouché's need for educated help with this work provided the opening for what was no doubt Lelièvre's first employment in America. With another Frenchman, Jean-Claude François Gonhot, he worked for five months from the fall of 1834 through the winter of 1835 to catalog the books and get the inventory in shape for a public sale.[22]

21. Succession of Charles Jourdan, Supplementary inventory of the estate of Charles Jourdan [by] H. Pedesclaux, N.P., Sept. 10, 1834, NONA.

22. Succession of Charles Jourdan, Court of Probates for the Parish of Orleans, 1834, (New Orleans Public Library [hereafter NOPL], Louisiana Division), microfilm roll 116.

As Xavier Fouché struggled in court over the administration of Charles Jourdan's estate, the absent heirs challenged the level of compensation owed to Lelièvre and Gonhot. The very week of Lelièvre's February letter to his brother in France, Fouché was defending the amount in court. Much work and skill had been needed, he argued, to organize and create an auction catalog for the vast inventory that was spilling out of drawers, armoires, and vitrines throughout the shop, from the little subscription reading room in the back to the front windows overlooking Royal Street.[23]

The matter was not resolved until November of 1836, when Probate Judge Joachim Bermudez overruled the opposition, confirmed Fouché's accounts, and closed the succession. By that time Lelièvre's prospects had changed for the better. Just three months after his plaintive letter home, he became engaged to marry Virginie Fouché, Xavier's sister and part heir to the bookstore. No doubt they had met right in the shop where he was employed and she had lived with her uncle as a young abandoned wife. Surely they had marveled that their home towns of Gavray and Caen were a scant fifty miles apart across the fertile valleys of Normandy. As events played out, nearly one year after Lelièvre's July 1834 arrival in New Orleans, he married Virginie, with Xavier as a witness, and some friends gathered around.[24]

Lelièvre and his wife had been married about six months when Xavier Fouché suddenly died.[25] A year earlier, Fouché had formed a part-

23. Succession of Charles Jourdan, Inventory of the estate of Charles Jourdan, H. Pedesclaux, N.P., June 4–9, 1834, NONA.

24. Marriage contract, Lelièvre and V. Fouché, Carlile Pollock, N.P., June 23, 1835, NONA. Virginie Fouché's first marriage was to Joseph Mazzoti (Christoval de Armas, N.P., December 5, 1818, NONA). Among the friends were Paul Lacroix, a merchant, and Francois Fleischbein, a portrait painter from Bavaria (Carlile Pollock, N.P., June 23, 1835, NONA).

25. Court of Probates for the Parish of Orleans, records of 1836, NOPL, Louisiana Division.

nership with Jean-Claude Gonhot, the coworker, to own and operate the bookstore jointly, but he had also written a will leaving his estate to his sister.[26] This left Virginie Fouché Lelièvre with half of the business at the time of her brother's death. A few months later Lelièvre bought out the partner, to achieve with his wife full control of the bookstore.[27] Two years after that, thirty-six-year-old Virginie Fouché Lelièvre herself died childless, leaving a will bequeathing her entire estate to her husband.[28] It was now September 1838. Jacques-Felix Lelièvre, age forty-three and a four-year resident of the city, found himself sole owner of the bookstore, lending library, and stationer's business "founded in 1800"[29] by Charles Jourdan at the busy intersection of Royal and St. Ann Streets in the heart of the old French section of New Orleans.

II. Books and Book Selling in Antebellum New Orleans

It was not a bad time to be in business in New Orleans, specifically in the business of selling French books and stationery supplies. The city was growing, and business was good. Its population would more than double during the decade of Lelièvre's arrival, from some 46,000 to over 102,000. Many of the newcomers were Frenchmen with a strong attachment to their native country. This feeling was also still strong among the Creole population. French literature played its part in the Anglo-French struggle for cultural ascendancy that formed the chief platform of local politics in this period, creating a market for both new works and new editions of classics in French. Creoles also evidently pre-

26. Carlile Pollock, N.P., April 23, 25, 1835, NONA.

27. L. Feraud, N.P., March 11, 1836, NONA.

28. Carlile Pollock, N.P., April 10, 1838, NONA.

29. City directories in later years would carry advertisements that the Lelièvre bookstore was "founded in 1800."

ferred to buy stationery supplies and even toys and games made in France rather than in America. These included everything from packets of letter paper and bottles of ink to pens and pencils, framed writing slates, playing cards, toy guns, and knives. There was also a good market for French textbooks; curricular packets; French, Spanish, and Latin dictionaries; romances; Catholic devotional books; and highly decorative French-language holy cards.[30]

Of course, Lelièvre's was not the only book and stationery store in town. Jourdan, his predecessor, had numerous competitors through the years, among them Philadelphian Pierre Roche and later Roche's widow and sons. Also in the business were Mary Carroll, an Irishwoman who primarily sold English-language books and periodicals; Camille and Gaston Bruslé, printers and booksellers who had once rented in Jourdan's house; the New Yorker Benjamin Levy, who combined the businesses of bookseller, printer, and publisher in the American sector; and the bookseller Fourcade and his wife in the Vieux Carré. Jourdan's nearest competitor, however, was perhaps Antoine Louis Boimare, a Sorbonne-educated bibliophile with a personality somewhat like Jourdan's. Jourdan and Boimare had even once tried a partnership, no doubt because they both drew on the world of French ideas. Neither Jourdan nor Boimare was much suited to partnerships, however—especially with people similar to themselves—and their brief association, begun in May 1822, ended with a series of lawsuits filed just six months after it began.[31]

30. *Charles Jourdan v A. L. Boimare,* 1JDC 6079, NOPL.

31. John M. Goudeau, "Booksellers and Printers in New Orleans, 1764–1885," *Journal of Library History* 5, no. 1 (1970): 9; Florence M. Jumonville, "Books, Libraries, and Undersides for the Skies of Beds: The Extraordinary Career of A. L. Boimare," *Louisiana History* 34, no. 4 (1993): 441–42. The affair commenced when Jourdan sold his business to Boimare and a partner in May 1822, probably a convenient arrangement so Jourdan could return to France to buy books. The price of the business and its lease was

Papers from the lawsuits, along with estate inventories, reveal much about Creole literary interests in the antebellum period. It was de rigeur to have seventeenth- and eighteenth-century French classics from the golden ages of Louis XIV and of Voltaire and Rousseau. Creoles also collected a certain core group of lighter works. Responding to this market, Jourdan shipped home from an 1822 sojourn in France some thirty baled shipments of books acquired from his Parisian sources, chiefly Bossange Frères and the publisher Alexis Eymèry. Bossange Frères shipped works of Rousseau, Fenelon, Mesdames de Sévigné and de Maintenon, La Fontaine, Corneille, Montesquieu, Pascal, Boileau, and a number of other seventeenth- and eighteenth-century French writers. Other titles were from more obscure authors who were evidently quite popular. The core group invariably included Jean-Jacques Barthélemy's *Voyage du jeune Anacharsis en Grèce, dans le milieu du quatrième siècle avant l'ère vulgaire,* better known as *Le Jeune Anacharsis.* Jourdan probably ordered the 1821 edition of this seven-volume work, which was first published in Paris in 1788. Another title then popular but now obscure was a philosophical history by Constantin-François Volney, *Les Ruines; ou, meditation sur les revolutions des empires.* Better known as Volney's *Ruines,* this book was first published in Geneva in 1791 and would see

---

a steep $18,000, but the shop was in a prominent Royal Street building owned by the wardens of St. Louis Cathedral in an area frequented by Roman Catholics who could be expected to patronize the religious inventory. Boimare, however, was young and newly arrived in New Orleans and was slow to make payments. The agreement had a further setback when the partner died a few months later. Although Boimare found another partner the following winter, he still had not fulfilled his purchase agreement. Jourdan and Boimare attempted a settlement in June 1823, which initially avoided a lawsuit while Jourdan returned to France a second time. Once in Paris, however, Jourdan drew notes on the store in New Orleans and later refused to honor the drafts, forcing Boimare to pay them. The lawsuits that inevitably followed yielded to history a summary of their business operations and the first of five known inventories of the Jourdan—later Lelièvre—bookstore, three of which have been located to date (*Jourdan v Boimare*).

its tenth edition by 1832. Creoles also loved such comedies as *Monsieur Botte, Enfans du Carnaval,* and *Les Barons de Felsheim,* by Pigault-Le-Brun, whose works no doubt have not been staged in a century. The poetical works of Evariste Desire de Forges Parny in five-volume sets were also necessary to the Creole library. Jourdan shipped six sets of Parny in 1822. Finally, Jourdan was careful to carry French translations of three great classics: Plutarch's *Lives, Les Mille et un Nuits (Thousand and One Nights),* and Cervantes' *Don Quixote.*[32]

Among the few English works Jourdan shipped to New Orleans in 1822 were Goldsmith's *History of Greece* and two sixty-one volume sets of the works of Walter Scott. Jourdan also carried a large inventory of French-English and Spanish-English dictionaries, as would Lelièvre in his day. The most enduring of these were the compilations of Abel Boyer, which appeared in forty or more editions during the eighteenth and nineteenth centuries. Other important dictionaries were those of Francisco Sobrino, Pierre-Claude Victoire Boiste, and the French Academy. Bossange Frères had published a revised edition of the Academy dictionary in 1814. Another popular reference work was the *Vocabulaire* of Alfred de Wally. These books cost as much as five dollars, some fifty times the price of a romance novel or a devotional book.[33]

Titles aimed specifically at women and girls included *Les Etudes convenables aux demoiselles,* which in two volumes instructed young women in boarding schools about correct grammar, poetry, rhetoric, letter writing, morality, and rules of charity. *Conseils à ma fille* by Jean-Nicolas Bouilly rendered advice. The six-volume *Lettres à Emily* by Charles-Albert Demoustier taught mythology. Young mothers could purchase *Modestie de sa jeunesse, Modestie des jeunes personnes, Héloise et Abelard,* or *Les Jeunes Enfants.* Finally, ladies who preferred to read women writ-

32. *Jourdan v Boimare.*
33. *Ibid.*

ers could choose a novel such as *Elisabeth* by Mme Sophie Cottin, the *Lettres* of Mme Ninon de l'Enclos, or a book of fairy tales compiled by Marie Catherine d'Aulnoy.[34]

Works on art, science, and architecture were scarce, but Jourdan did ship Jean-Nicholas Durand's two-volume *Cours d'Architecture* and a work invoices referred to as *La Maison Rustique.* The full title was *Maison Rustique du XIX siècle: encyclopedie d'agriculture practique et de jardinage.* This journal, alternately entitled *Le Bon Jardinier,* would be an important source book for Lelièvre fifteen years later. Perhaps related to it was the *Manuel d'économie rurale,* author unknown.

These kinds of books, along with prints, maps, toys, and stationery supplies formed the shop that Lelièvre acquired by purchase and inheritance during his first years in New Orleans. These were the types of books in the 1834 inventory of Charles Jourdan's estate,[35] and similar items could still be found in the store twenty years later at Lelièvre's own death. They were there because they were in demand, and by fostering French intellectual life in antebellum New Orleans they contributed to the demand for more books newly published or republished in France. Did they sell? Yes. Jourdan's accounts in 1822 showed that the store had about three thousand dollars per quarter in sales, including nonbook inventory. Considering that the most expensive item in the store was a five dollar dictionary and that most books sold for less than fifty cents, unit sales must have been brisk.[36]

Inventories of private libraries in Louisiana show that the French bought these kinds of books. The much-studied library of Pointe Coupée planter Vincent Ternant Jr. at Parlange Plantation, for example,

34. *Ibid.*

35. H. Pedesclaux, N.P., June 3, 1834, NONA.

36. *"Compte-rendu de la gestion faite par A. L. Boimare des affaires de Mr. Chs. Jourdan, pendant son voyage en France depuis le 1.er Juin jusqu'au 25 December 1823," Jourdan v Boimare.*

contained the *Travels of Anacharsis*, the works of Fenelon, the *Fables* of La Fontaine, the *Letters to Emily*, the dictionaries of Boyer and of the French Academy, the works of Parny, the French version of the *Lives* of Plutarch, the works of Walter Scott, *Héloise and Abelard*, Volney's *Ruines*, and numerous other classics, when inventoried in 1842.[37] Marie Elizabeth Boré Gayarré, who died twenty years earlier, had similar interests. This quintessential Creole was the daughter of Louisiana sugar pioneer Etienne Boré, the daughter-in-law of the Spanish royal comptroller Estevan Gayarré, and the mother of New Orleans historian Charles Gayarré. Her library was full of Greek classics in French and abounded in seventeenth- and eighteenth-century French literature. Madame Gayarré had whole sets of Rousseau, Corneille, Boileau, Montesquieu, Chateaubriand, Mme de Sévigné, Mme de Maintenon, and many others. The Creoles' core favorites were also represented—Parny's poetry; Pigault-LeBrun's comedies; the *Voyage d'Anacharsis;* and the *Lettres à Emilie.*[38]

Another important private library was that of Dr. Yves Lemonnier, a native of Rennes who emigrated to New Orleans in 1809 after fleeing the revolution in St. Domingue and living for a time in Santiago, Cuba. LeMonnier managed to overcome the difficulties of transporting his library from St. Domingue to Cuba and eventually to New Orleans, where he kept it in his mansion at the corner of Royal and St. Peter Streets. Lemonnier devoted the greatest single part of his library to professional works—in this case medical books—but he too collected French fiction. He had the works of the seventeenth-century French classicists such as La Fontaine and Molière and six volumes of the novels of Sophie Cottin. His French reference works included the one-

---

37. Walter R. Patrick and Cecil G. Taylor, "A Louisiana French Plantation Library, 1842," *French-American Review* (January–March 1948): 47–67.

38. H. Lavergne, N.P., January 23, 1823, NONA.

hundred-volume *Dictionnaire des Sciences Naturelles,* a fifty-two-volume *Biographie Universelle,* and nearly two thousand issues of the *Almanach de Commerce.* A graduate of the French Academy of Surgery, Dr. Lemonnier had its seven-volume *Prix de l'Academie* among his most valuable possessions. One supposes that in view of its several relocations, his library was probably much larger at one time, but it still contained several hundred books and thousands of periodicals at the time of his death in 1832.[39]

One of the greatest private libraries of the antebellum period in New Orleans was that of the Creole notary Michel de Armas, kept at his home and office on Chartres Street in the Vieux Carré just four blocks from Jourdan's bookstore. De Armas owned several thousand books in French, English, Spanish, Latin, Italian, and Greek at the time of his death in September 1823. Because of his notarial and legal practice, about a third of the library consisted of legal books such as civil law treatises, digests, and court reports, but he also owned the literary types similar to the books that Charles Jourdan shipped from Paris in 1822.[40]

In these private libraries and evidently in the Jourdan bookstore, books on horticulture were scarce. Michel de Armas' library contained only one horticultural title among some thirty-five hundred books, the two-volume *Jeune Botaniste.* The sole horticultural work identified among Jourdan's 1822 invoices was the *Maison Rustique.* There was also a book on chemistry by Chaptal, which could have been his famous soil treatise *Chymie appliqué à l'agriculture.* The Ternant inventory had no gardening titles. LeMonnier's collection was something of an exception because medical education in his day was strong in botany and the medicinal qualities of plants. His library had at least six titles relating to

39. Inventory of the estate of Dr. Yves Lemonnier, Octave de Armas, N.P., July 19, 1832, NONA.

40. H. Lavergne, N.P., September 20, 1823, NONA.

horticulture, including *Plantes de Ste. Domingue;*[41] Chaptal's two-volume *Chimie appliqué à l'agriculture; Botanique Médicale* in three volumes; *Leçons de Flore,* two volumes; and the most important work on classifying species, *Système de Linné.* Most of these, however, were related to classifying plants or using them in a medicinal context rather than to growing vegetables, fruits, and ornamentals.

It was thus to fill a real need that Jacques-Felix Lelièvre composed and published *Nouveau Jardinier de la Louisiane* in 1838. He directly expressed his feeling that there would be merit in an experienced grower issuing a work adapted to the climate of Louisiana and aimed at those working in *jardinage*—the growing of vegetables, fruit, and ornamental plants as opposed to large-scale agriculture or plants grown for science and medicine. Lelièvre held the great multivolume works of the Abbé Rozier and his colleagues and those of the Institute of France in great respect, but theirs were not the kinds of books that one could put in his back pocket when stepping outside with the hoe. For the needs of those who "wished to direct the works in their garden themselves," Lelièvre noted, he had "determined to compose this book."[42]

The writer's assessment was valid. There was no gardening guide adapted to a climate like that of Louisiana, with the possible exception of Lemonnier's *Plantes de St. Domingue,* which was probably in the genre of a *flore* (list of plants in a specified area). It was also indisputable that the great French works were "too voluminous" to use as handbooks. Still, one suspects that there was more at work in all this—and that which was at work was all in English. Twenty years earlier, John Gardiner had published *The American Gardener* at Georgetown in Washington, D.C., with a subtitle proclaiming his product's usefulness

41. Author not given; some candidates are Charles Plumier, Louis Dutour, Jean-Baptiste Poupée Desportes, and Jean Damier Chevalier.

42. *Nouveau Jardinier de la Louisiane* (New Orleans: Librairie de J. F. Lelièvre, 1838), v.

for cultivating kitchen gardens, flowers, vineyards, and more. As early as 1806, Bernard M'Mahon had begun publishing *The American Gardener's Calendar,* which claimed to be adapted to all of the climates and seasons in the United States and was in its seventh edition by 1828. Thomas G. Fessender had produced *The New American Gardener* in 1828, emphasizing fruits and vegetables, the science of pruning and hoeing, making slips, grafting, and so on. And Robert Buist had written a book of practical directions for garden plants, hothouse construction, layouts, soil, seeds, and every kind of horticultural tip for each month of the year.[43] These books were written in English, had been published in Philadelphia, Boston, or New York, and were tantalizingly successful.

Did those titles get to New Orleans? Some did. New Orleans banker John Linton by 1834 had both *The American Gardener* and *The New American Gardener* in his library.[44] Samuel Bannister Slocomb, who had a large dry goods and hardware store on Canal Street, offered books in English on chemistry and medicine—two subjects that touched on horticultural issues at the time—amid his basins, patent balances, and fly wheels.[45] And farther into the American sector across Canal Street from the Vieux Carré, the competition was fierce. Clustered near the fashion-

43. *American Flower-Garden Directory: Containing Practical Directions for the Culture of Plants/in the Flower Garden, Hot-House, Green-House, Rooms, or Parlor Windows, For Every Month in the Year. With A Description of the Plants Most Desirable in Each, the Nature of the Soil, and Situation Best Adapted to their Growth, The Proper Season for Transplanting, etc. With Instructions for Erecting A Hot-House, Green-House, and Laying Out a Flower-Garden. The Whole Adapted to Either Large or Small Gardens. With Instructions for Preparing the Soil, Propagating, Planting, Pruning, Training and Fruiting the Grapevine. With Descriptions of the Best Sorts For Cultivating in the Open Air. Fourth Edition, with Numerous Additions. By Robert Buist, Nurseryman and Seed Grower* (Philadelphia: A. Hart, 1851).

44. Inventory of the estate of John Linton, H. B. Cenas, N.P., October 3, 1834, NONA.

45. H. B. Cenas, N.P., September 26, 1834, NONA.

able St. Charles hotel was a nucleus of printers, booksellers, office suppliers, and seedsmen's stores, among them that of William Dinn, an ambitious seedsman and florist on Common Street. Dinn widely advertised his garden, farm, and flower seeds; his garden tools and agricultural implements; his fruit trees, shrubbery, greenhouse plants, and "Dutch bulbous flower roots"; and his books on gardening, farming, and the culture of silk, all in English.[46]

The centuries-old struggle between England and France played out once more in the New Orleans of the pre–Civil War period. Thousands of Americans settled in New Orleans after the Louisiana Purchase to make their fortunes or just to find a better life in a vibrant city. There they encountered thousands of Francophone Creoles and French immigrants. The battle was joined over issues relating to the legal system, i.e., whether Louisiana would follow civil or common law; over cultural issues such as the relative popularity of French and American theaters, dramas, music, plays, and operas; in the struggle between Catholicism and Protestantism; in politics, of course; and especially in the area of what was to be the prevailing language in New Orleans. Political issues played out to a large degree in 1836—just two years after Lelièvre's arrival—when the city split into three municipal subdivisions, two Creole and one Anglo, each having a council and executive officers, under a single mayor. This experiment ended with a compromise in 1852, but the struggle to preserve a French-inspired way of life was still alive as late as 1925 in New Orleans.

As a true Frenchman and one who knew scientific gardening, Lelièvre was quick to perceive the role he could play in meeting a need for a gardening manual in French. Was this to meet the competition in English? The title and the circumstances suggest it. If there was a *New American Gardener,* certainly there could be a *New Louisiana Gardener.*

---

46. Pitts and Clark, *New Orleans City Directory,* 1842.

There was a strong precedent for booksellers in New Orleans to function also as publishers, just as they did in Paris. Charles Jourdan had an old press in his shop and as early as 1818 had published a catechism for the Reverend Père Antoine, the popular rector of St. Louis Cathedral. The book contained a frontispiece that read in part "Chez Ch. Jourdan, Libraire, rue Sainte-Anne, 1818."[47] As late as 1834, he still had the volume for sale on his bookshelves.[48] Florence M. Jumonville has noted that Jourdan's competitor A. L. Boimare published at least seventeen works between 1826 and 1832, some in partnership with the French civil engineer Benjamin Buisson.[49] Roche Frères, booksellers, also published at least one book of their own, *Elemens de la grammaire française,* and won printing contracts from the Bank of Louisiana, the Louisiana Legislature, and the Louisiana Supreme Court. Alfred Moret, a friend, customer, and business associate of Jourdan, also did some publishing in New Orleans before Lelièvre's time.[50] And so it was natural for Lelièvre, bookseller, to step into publishing. He simply began with the subject he knew best.

III. Nouveau Jardinier de la Louisiane

In its own small way, *Nouveau Jardinier de la Louisiane* promulgated the theories of early modern botanical science as it had developed in France

47. *Abrégé du Catechisme de la Louisiane . . . Nouvelle ed., Approuvé. Par le Très Révérend Père Antoine de Sedella, Curé de l'église paroissale de la Nouvelle Orléans.* Historic New Orleans Collection.

48. Jourdan inventory, H. Pedesclaux, N.P., 1834, NONA.

49. Jumonville, "Boimare," 445.

50. A number of Roche Frères' imprints are in the collection of Howard-Tilton Memorial Library, Tulane University. On Moret, see testimony of Moret, Succession of Charles Jourdan; see also Moret's *La Famille Creole, drame en cinq actes et en prose* by Auguste Lussan (New Orleans: Chez Frémaux et Alfred Moret, 1837).

during the late seventeenth, eighteenth, and early nineteenth centuries. The 150 years before Lelièvre's time had been a period of intense research and discovery in European botanical studies, especially in France, where botany was à la mode among the educated classes. In Paris, the great Georges-Louis LeClerc, Comte de Buffon and director of the *Jardin du Roi,* applied his considerable influence to the introduction of scientific investigation into natural phenomena. For two centuries the Garden and the French Marine were institutional sponsors in sending botanists throughout the world to find and retrieve thousands of new species to be studied and propagated back home. It was within this context that botanist André Michaux explored the eastern part of the United States and exchanged specimens between France and his Carolina nursery.[51]

The *Nouveau Jardinier* was also a vehicle for the eighteenth-century French Enlightenment. Through their publications, Jean-Jacques Rousseau, Denis Diderot, and the school of the Encyclopedists had popularized a scientific approach to life in general and material arts in particular as a means of promoting progress for mankind. Scientific horticulture was one method of achieving that progress for the common man. One precept was to apply the principles of astronomy to discern which seasons and phases of the moon were best for planting. Thus gardening manuals such as the *Nouveau Jardinier* contained both an almanac and some rather abstruse astronomical lessons such as the calculations for the "epact," the "golden number," and the "dominical letter." These explanations, along with their accompanying calendar of saints' days, consume the entire first chapter of Lelièvre's text. Strange as the presentation is to us today, we must understand its role in strong opposition to what its proponents considered the "foolish" use of astronomy to predict the affairs of men.[52]

51. De Virville, *Histoire,* 6–7; Duval, *King's Garden,* 99–132.
52. Rozier, ed., *Cours complet d'agriculture,* 1:365.

One of the scientists who espoused this scientific approach to horticulture and actually conducted experiments instead of simply reading about them was the Abbé François Rozier of Lyons. Rousseau visited Rozier during the 1760s and learned much from him about herbiary and botany. The abbé and several other scientists were working to compile the *Cours Complet d'Agriculture* when the French Revolution broke out. Although Rozier met death from a bomb during the siege of Lyons in the fall of 1793 just after the first volume appeared, the series continued and carried on the work of the Enlightenment as it pertained to horticulture.[53]

It is clear both from Lelièvre's introductory remarks and from his text that Lelièvre subscribed to the philosophy of horticultural progress pioneered by Enlightenment writers and carried forward by Rozier, Chaptal, Thouin, and others. It was a kind of progress that the ordinary man could achieve through knowledge of such matters as proper plowing, scientific grafting, the skilled use of the *taille* (structured pruning) to increase fruit production, and the modification of frigid climatic influences through manured hotbeds, greenhouses, the reflective heat of brick walls, and the use of *clôches* (glass domes). Rozier and his fellow writers addressed these subjects in the *Cours Complet,* as did the Agricultural Section of the Institute of France when revising the work some years later. Lelièvre in turn took them up, proposing his own climatic modifications to suit Louisiana. Plants not cultivated in that region, he wrote, could be cultivated there with success, "the richness of the soil permitting all expectations when the plants that one confines to it are managed according to wisely combined principles of cultivation."[54]

This fundamental belief that the well-informed Louisiana gardener could overcome the problems of heat, humidity, weeds, insects, occa-

53. *Ibid.,* v.
54. *Nouveau Jardinier,* v–vi.

sional cold, and primitive species by scientific methods of providing shade, water, and drainage; by scientific pruning, manuring, and plowing; and through grafting, budding, and layering of better species onto native stock—with the timing all regulated by the study of astronomy and an understanding of the movement of sap—was at the heart of his book. Lelièvre was in the vanguard of the optimistic spirit of the French *cultivateurs marâichères* (market gardeners) who by 1860 would achieve fame throughout Europe for their prize specimens and particularly early crops of fruits and vegetables and by 1890 had become the specific envy of British growers.[55] The movement to address and alter climatic limitations was the inspiration for Lelièvre's suggestions that Louisiana growers could grow drought-loving lavender in humid New Orleans and succeed with green peas in May; with lettuce, radishes, peas, and beans in June; and with parsley, spinach, and the curly Savoy cabbage throughout the summer.

Lelièvre placed a high priority on vegetables. He emphasized them more than he did ornamentals, about which he knew less. Viewed in the light of the nineteenth-century American food production system, this emphasis was normal for a manual. Robert F. Becker has quoted the nineteenth-century horticulturist Charles Hovey, who wrote in *The Gardener's Magazine* in 1835 that contemporary city dwellers could find tomatoes, celery, cauliflower, broccoli, and hothouse vegetables in their markets, an achievement for that period. According to Becker, by 1835 "the major cities of the United States were being supplied with quantities of fresh produce from skilled professional market gardeners [who] farmed at the very edges of the major cities, raising high-value, perish-

55. W. Robinson, *Gleanings from French Gardens, Comprising an Account of such Features of French Horticulture as Are Most Worthy of Adoption in British Gardens,* 2nd ed. (London, Frederick Warne, 1869); Thomas Smith, *French Gardening* (London, 1909); John Weathers, *French Market-Gardening, Including Practical Details of "Intensive Cultivation" for English Growers* (London, 1909).

able crops on land that was relatively expensive. They used intensive production practices and produced a mix of crops that generated the greatest possible return per acre. To . . . prolong the fall growing season, overwinter tender perennials, and force plants in winter, market gardeners constructed cold frames, hot beds, and after about 1870, glass houses."[56]

Traditionally, the market gardeners serving the New Orleans area resided on truck farms in the upriver parishes of Jefferson, St. Charles, St. John the Baptist, and St. James and downriver in St. Bernard and Plaquemines Parishes, where there were extensive orange groves. But Lelièvre's intended audience no doubt also included the market gardener of what was then suburban New Orleans, equivalent to Becker's "very edge of a major city." During the 1830s, this would have included the areas immediately downriver from the Vieux Carré and upriver from the American sector (today's Central Business District). In these sections the underlying plantations of the eighteenth century had been broken up and redeveloped, some as independent towns and some as faubourgs. The faubourg was literally a "false town," a quasi city where, at least on paper, there were streets and squares but no state-granted municipal charters bestowing local police or taxing powers. The earliest faubourgs—Ste. Marie, Annunciation, Marigny, Tremé, and St. John— were close to town and soon part of the city. By 1838 New Orleans also had two independently incorporated suburbs, the city of Lafayette and the town of Carrollton. Lafayette, annexed in 1852, is now the Garden District. Carrollton, at the river bend some five miles above the city limits and annexed in 1874, is now the Carrollton neighborhood. There were also rural sections "back of town," below and lakeward from the

56. Robinson, *Gleanings;* Smith, *French Gardening;* Weathers, *French Market-Gardening;* Robert F. Becker, "Gardening for Profit: Supplying America's Cities with Vegetables Prior to 1900," in *Proceedings of the 1990 Annual Meeting,* Association for Living Historical Farms and Agricultural Museums, 138–41.

Faubourgs Marigny and Tremé, and on the opposite bank of the Mississippi. In these outlying sections the New Orleans grower of the 1830s spread out his plots in squares or rows to grow produce, cover *tonnelles* (arbors) with scuppernong grapes or scarlet runner bean, operate dairies, or bake French bread. He kept his own horses and stables on site and delivered his products by wagon to the French Market in the Vieux Carré, to the Washington Market just below the Faubourg Marigny, or to the American sector's St. Mary and Poydras Markets. Lelièvre's intent was in part to address these growers, to make them more professional. He wanted to share the riches of French scientific horticulture with his adopted region.[57]

One might note again that Lelièvre's stated target was the gardener "directing his works himself." This probably included both the market farmer and the middle-class or gentleman gardener with a "suburban villa," one of the large galleried houses surrounded by gardens and dependencies and usually occupying two adjacent squares on one of the major thoroughfares such as St. Charles Avenue. Archival drawings have left us numerous views of these sumptuous period estates carved out of newly subdivided plantations adjacent to the city. With their dependent kitchens, servants' buildings, chicken houses, cisterns, gazebos, avenues of trees, *potagers* (vegetable gardens), and formal parterres, they looked something like plantations, but lacked large-scale agricultural features. They did not produce a cash crop other than fruits and vegetables and did not include rows of slave quarters like those found on plantation estates of the South. As the term implies, they were essentially suburban rather than rural.

Lelièvre purposely did not design his book for *culture en grand* (large-

57. For a discussion of the spread of public markets in New Orleans, see Robert A. Sauder, "The Origin and Spread of the Public Market System in New Orleans," *Louisiana History* 22, no. 3 (1981): 281–97.

scale agriculture). In a society of plantations worked by ample crews of slaves, he did not aim his work at the grower of sugar or cotton. The word "slave" does not appear in his monograph. Nor has evidence been found among numerous documents pertaining to his life that he ever owned any slaves. He fits, in short, the pattern of the liberal nineteenth-century French intellectual or scientist.

Nineteenth-century French horticultural science also formed the background of the *Nouveau Jardinier* from a literary viewpoint. Lelièvre was less knowledgeable about ornamentals than he was about vegetables, and he was obviously not averse to borrowing descriptions for them. The author's specific literary source for his discussion of ornamental flowers was the 1836 edition of *Le Bon Jardinier,* an annual horticultural encyclopedia of some one thousand pages that had been published in Paris since 1755. The *Bon Jardinier* was dedicated to the regular publishing of advances in the science of horticulture. Over the years, a series of the most prominent horticulturists of France had edited it, men such as Thomas-François De Grace, Mordant de Launay, Louis Noisette, the nurseryman Vinache, M. Pirolle, and others. The format included a hagiographic almanac (calendar of saints' feast days), articles on new plant varieties and imports, reports on major flower shows of the day (for example, large dahlia shows in Brussels), announcements about new publications, a calendar of monthly garden tasks, general discussions of soil and gardening principles, and—the heart of each volume—about seventeen hundred individual entries on vegetables, fruits, and flowers. For each plant the journal identified both botanical and common French names; described the stalk, leaves, and flowers; and gave instructions for its cultivation and propagation.[58]

From these flower lists Lelièvre borrowed generously, shortening the entries, changing a word here and there, moving a phrase, omitting,

58. *Le Bon Jardinier* (1836).

summarizing, or closely paraphrasing long discussions, and completely omitting foliar descriptions and botanical names. His primary changes related to the recommended time of sowing and transplanting, the length of entries, and the selection of plants. To illustrate, the table below compares the two entries for celosia.

Bon Jardinier	*Nouveau Jardinier*
Célosie à Crète, Amaranthe des jardiniers Crête-de-Coq. . . . Celosia cristata. L.	*Célosie; crête de coq*
Tiges de 2 pieds [stem 2 feet]	*Tiges de 2 pieds* [stem 2 feet]
fleurs trés-petites, tellement nombreuses, et serrées en tête longues, applaties et plissées [very small flowers, somewhat numerous, and serrated in long heads, flattened and folded]	*fleurs petites, nombreuses, serrées, en têtes longues, applaties en crête* [small flowers, numerous, serrated, with long heads, flattened into crests]
Semer en mars sur couche, mettre en terre avec la motte [Plant in March in hotbed, put into the ground with the clump of soil]	*Semer en avril en bonne terre ou en mars sur couche, transplanter avec la motte.* [Plant in April in good earth or in March in hotbed, transplant in clump of soil.]
Preserver du moindre froid [Protect from the slightest cold]	*Elle craint le froid* [It is averse to cold]

Sources: *Le Bon Jardinier* (1836), 583; *Nouveau Jardinier*, 162.

Lelièvre borrowed from the *Bon Jardinier* in this pattern for most of the ninety or so ornamental plants that he included. This model provided firm ground for the translator to include corresponding botanical names from the obviously plagiarized source, although not all entries were parallel. An example is Lelièvre's entry for *chèvrefeuille* (honeysuckle). While both he and the *Bon Jardinier* treated it as a family of eight genera, Lelièvre also provided his own stem, flower, and propagation notes. The plant had a sweet aroma, he noted, and was very good for covering arbors and providing shade. Lelièvre's entries for wall-flower, jasmine, morning glory, poinciana, sunflower, tulip, verbena, violet, and red-flowered zinnia were also original.

As for the plagiarism, there was ample precedent. Historian Brenda Bullion has pointed out that Robert Squibb's 1787 *Gardener's Calendar for South Carolina, Georgia and North Carolina* borrowed extensively from Londoner John Abercrombie's *Every Man in His Own Garden,* published twenty years earlier. For the 1804 *American Gardener,* she notes, authors John Gardiner and David Hepburn "relied heavily on the plant lists of John Abercrombie who, in turn, based his lists directly on those in [Philip] Miller's *Gardener's Kalendar.*" In spite of their borrowing, Bullion characterizes the manual of Gardiner and Hepburn as credible for the study of early nineteenth-century conditions in North America.[59]

If the borrowing makes Lelièvre's work seem less valuable as a witness to the state of ornamental horticulture in antebellum New Orleans, one might reflect that the author had considerable latitude in his choice of entries. While the *Bon Jardinier* treated seventeen hundred plants, Lelièvre discussed only ninety ornamentals, fifty-two vegetables, and four kinds of fruit trees. He entitled the first chapter on individual plants "Cultivation of the Plants Most Used in Louisiana." He evidently judged it unnecessary to reinvent descriptions for species already described by writers better than he. Although less knowledgeable about ornamentals than about vegetables, Lelièvre devoted an entire page to making a case for growing flowers, as the cultivation of a large variety of ornamental plants did not yet enjoy widespread popularity in the average American garden in his day. "Flowers also merit the attention of the [garden] enthusiast," he urged. "They are the most beautiful orna-

59. Brenda Bullion, "Early American Farming and Gardening Literature: 'Adapted to the Climates and Seasons of the United States,'" *Journal of Garden History* 12, no. 1 (1992): 29.

ment of the garden." His selections are testimony to the ornamental plants that he either found in use in New Orleans or judged amenable to trying there.

While Lelièvre clearly borrowed his ornamental plant descriptions, there is some latitude to conclude that he composed his own entries for vegetables, and certainly he placed a higher priority on them. Lelièvre's vegetable entries differ significantly from the corresponding texts in various editions of the *Bon Jardinier,* his usual source for flowers, and from those in several other popular French gardening manuals of the day, such as Noisette's, Pirolle's, or that of Philippe Levêque de Vilmorin, a famous seed merchant in Paris (1746–1807) and founder of the still-operating business on the quai. While he probably used Noisette's *Manuel du Jardinier* as a frequent reference, perhaps borrowing ideas on pruning and grafting from it, his handling of the material relating to the growing of vegetables suggests personal knowledge of technique. Noisette, for example, mentions the alternative of growing watercress in water-filled tubs when a stream is lacking, but with scant explanation as to how to make it happen. Lelièvre also notes the tub alternative, but explains meticulously how to succeed with it. Overall, his discussions of vegetable growing are thorough, and it is probably safe to conclude that they constitute a fairly authentic mirror of *potager* management in New Orleans. At least one other source, an 1830 newspaper advertisement by a seed dealer on Royal Street about five blocks from Lelièvre's shop, bears out this theory. It provides evidence that at least twenty-nine of the vegetable species listed in the *Nouveau Jardinier* were available for sale even before Lelièvre's arrival. These included artichokes, asparagus, beets, cabbage, cauliflower, celery, carrots, cresses, chervil, cucumbers, eggplant, endive, leeks, beans, peas, lettuce, melons, and others.[60]

60. "Smith's Magasin de Graines," *Le Courrier de la Louisiane* (October 12, 1830). The other species listed were mustard, onions, parsley, parsnips, peppers, pumpkins, rad-

Do the book's assumptions about landscapes or even streetscapes command a similar presumption of accuracy? There is scant hint in the *Nouveau Jardinier* of the lushness that our generation has come to associate with "Old New Orleans" and similar Old South landscapes,[61] but Lelièvre could hardly have missed it. During his time of residence in the Vieux Carré, there were many courtyards near his shop laid out with narrow rectangular beds.[62] Service buildings containing kitchens and domestics' quarters usually flanked either a side or the rear of the yard. Occasionally a service building bisected the depth of the courtyard, dividing it into the *cour,* which was decorative, and the *basse-cour,* which was utilitarian. All of these areas had heavy vegetation, including such flowering shrubs as althea, agave, and banana, some of which are shown in period drawings in the collection of the Notarial Archives. The drawings, particularly those by Charles de Armas, a talented New Orleans Creole trained as a civil engineer, frequently indicate flower beds not shaded by trees, trees in rows (probably fruit trees), or trees as specimens, probably live oaks.[63] If the trees had overshadowed the beds, the

---

ishes, roquette, salsify, spinach, squash, turnips, and bird and grass seed. This list included more than one variety in most categories.The most numerous were lettuce (twelve varieties), cabbage (eight), and radishes and turnips (six each).

61. Suzanne Turner, "Roots of a Regional Garden Tradition: The Drawings of the New Orleans Notarial Archives," in *Regional Garden Design in the United States,* ed. Therese O'Malley and Marc Treib (Washington, D.C.: Dumbarton Oaks Research Library and Collection, 1995), 189.

62. Suzanne Turner and A. J. Meek, *The Gardens of Louisiana* (Baton Rouge: Louisiana State University Press, 1997), 4–6.

63. For more on Notarial Archives drawings, which were created pursuant to civil law rules for third-party notice in connection with judicial sales, see Sally K. Reeves, "The Plan Book Drawings of the New Orleans Notarial Archives: Legal Background and Artistic Development," in *The Cultivation of Artists in Nineteenth-Century America,* ed. Georgia Brady Barnhill, Diana Korzenik, and Caroline F. Sloat (Worcester, Mass.: American Antiquarian Society, 1997), 81–101.

yards would have had the predominantly green appearance that they have today rather than colorful flower beds. If the trees were small or closely clipped, there were probably many flowering plants, along with some vegetable beds in the *basse-cours.*

On the streets of the French Quarter there were few trees because of ditches and heavy mud overflow from ruts, but Lelièvre's shop overlooked a small square, the *Place St. Antoine,* located behind St. Louis Cathedral on Royal Street between Père Antoine's and St. Anthony's Alleys. The square was owned by the wardens of the cathedral, who leased space in it to small businesses, including an ice cream pavilion and a Parisian-style flower market. Here Courvoisier and Company sold flowers and shrubs grown on land in the Third Municipality in the Faubourg New Marigny and transported by wagon into town.[64]

Farther out in the suburbs, in the yard of the d'Estréhan home on the west bank of the Mississippi for example, there abounded "cape jasmines, oleanders, pittisporums, wild peach, crepe myrtles, woodbines, honey suckles, yellow jessamines, Japonicas, hydrangeas, violets, etc.," as a local teacher described it in 1846.[65] Of these, Lelièvre noted the camellia, hydrangea, oleander, honeysuckle, woodbine and violet—and he talked about covering arbors to create shade—but one gets a sense from his overall emphasis on vegetables, the pruning and grafting of fruit trees, and the scientific control of the environment, that his methods were not designed to promote, or even to come to grips with, the area's lush growth. Lelièvre's "new" Louisiana gardener, moreover, does not seem to deal with the overwhelming feature of the Louisiana landscape: *quercus virginiana,* the shady live oak, which frustrates the contemporary home gardener's efforts to grow flowers and vegetables.

64. A. Dreyfous, N.P., September 22, 1846, NONA. The little square, now fenced, is called "St. Anthony's Garden" today.

65. James L. Furman, *Reminiscences of an Octogenarian or the Autobiography of a School Teacher* (New Orleans: Office Baptist Visitor, 1904), 47–60.

Lelièvre's book most clearly mirrors the mind-set of nineteenth-century French horticultural science. Optimistic, ambitious, and progressive, it urged gardeners to manage nature by trying new species and constantly improving old ones through the application of new and better techniques. French gardening manuals and dictionaries of natural history were full of highly developed essays on a variety of gardening arts and sciences that readers were expected to try.[66] Of these, four were perhaps of greatest contemporary interest—the art of the *taille* (the correct pruning of fruit trees); the *greffe* (art of grafting); the identification of *terres* (soil types); and the use of the *serre* (greenhouse) to protect exotics from cold.

The art of the *taille* was as old as the Bible. Properly understood, it meant the correct pruning of vines and fruit trees, less for ornamental purposes than to increase production. In Leviticus the Lord said to Moses, "six years you shall sow your field, and six years *you shall prune your vineyard,* and gather in its fruits" (25:3, emphasis added). Fifteen hundred years later the Evangelist John quoted Jesus in a similar statement from the famous parable of the vine dresser: "I am the true vine, and my Father is the vine dresser. Every branch of mine that bears no fruit, he takes away, and every branch that does bear fruit he prunes, *that it may bear more fruit*" (John 15:1–7, emphasis added). The *taille,* from *tailler* (to cut, shape, or trim), is a complex procedure that involves identifying and encouraging fruit-producing buds and their subsequent branches while restricting wood buds. By 1800, French horticulturists were past masters of the *taille,* both for utility and for ornament. For over a century the gardens of Versailles had epitomized the use of highly structured pruning to achieve landscape effects, but thousands of ordi-

66. Louis Liger, *Le Jardinier fleuriste, ou la Culture universele des fleurs, arbres, arbustes* . . . (Paris, 1787); Louis Claude Noisette, *Manuel complet du jardinier, pépinièriste, botaniste* . . . (Brussels, 1829).

nary gardeners throughout the land were also skilled in the art for better winemaking and orchard management. Henri-Louis Duhamel du Monceau's eighteenth-century treatises on fruit trees and tree anatomies had promulgated his findings on the flow of sap and its management, which involved pruning to encourage fruit buds on trees while allowing wood buds only for proper maintenance of height and vigor.[67]

By the turn of the nineteenth century, André Thouin was the acknowledged expert on both the *taille* and the *greffe* and was managing the timing of the rise of sap in order to acclimate exotic species in Paris. In Thouin's time there was not a nation in the world in which more varieties of fruit trees were grown than in France—some eight hundred varieties from twenty-eight species. Thouin shared his knowledge of horticulture from his position as chief gardener of the *Jardin des Plantes* in Paris. There he experimented, demonstrated grafting and pruning techniques, and published instructions on how to increase and maintain output.[68]

Duhamel had made five divisions of graft types, identifying the *approche* (approach), *fente* (cleft), *couronne* (crown), *flute* (flute), and *écusson* (bud) types, each of which had numerous subdivisions. There were some 135 types in all, many named for their inventors. Thouin further analyzed the types, identifying those that united parts of trunks, branches, stems, or roots; those that separated ligneous parts from one specimen and placed them on another (subjects and scions); and those that united *gemmes* (eyes), lifting the eye with the portion of bark that surrounds it and putting it onto another specimen.[69] In the end it was thus less Lelièvre's task to find sources on the *taille* and the *greffe* than it was to shorten and summarize reams of published material and make it available in a handy format.

---

67. *Traité des arbres fruitiers contenant leur figure, leur descriptions* . . . (Paris, 1768).

68. *Dictionnaire d'Histoire Naturelle*, 2:154, 155–93; de Virville, *Histoire*, 99.

69. Noisette, *Manuel complet du jardinier*, 206–55, esp. 215.

Lelièvre may have summarized, but the intellectual leadership on improving species through the *greffe* and the *taille* to which he was heir shows clearly in the *Nouveau Jardinier*. This context explains his somewhat impatient introductory essay on the cultivation of fruit trees in lower Louisiana "below Baton Rouge and Pointe Coupée." He characterized these trees as "*très négligés,*" a rather puzzling indictment in light of Louisiana's century-old orange industry and the climate's abundance of figs, pomegranates, persimmons, and pear trees. "Even the oranges," Lelièvre wrote, "hardly produce here."[70]

The problem in Louisiana was that occasional but regular dips of the mercury below freezing usually killed the orange trees, forcing growers to start over again. This happened to all the orange groves of lower Louisiana in the freeze of February 20, 1823, as planter Nicholas Noel d'Estréhan recorded in his diary.[71] Lelièvre's remark about the trees "hardly producing" may seem unfair, but only until one reads Thouin on the subject of grafting orange trees. Thouin urged his readers never to wait until the orange tree matured (some eight years) to expect fruit, when one could hasten the era of fructification by cleft grafting a flowering branch onto a young trunk of two or three years. This technique even had a name, *greffe en fente à oranger.*[72]

If Thouin was the expert in pruning, grafting, and the naturalization of imported species, Chaptal was the leader in the chemical analysis of soils. From his work proceeded such French-language gardening conceits as *terre franche, terre forte,* and *terre de bruyère* (balanced, heavy, and peat-based soils) found in French manuals. This includes the *Nouveau Jardinier,* where the reader's understanding of these phrases is assumed. *Terre franche,* literally "free soil," technically meant soil that was

70. *Nouveau Jardinier,* 130.

71. Nicholas Noel d'Estréhan, "Naissances, Mortalités, et autres Notes," diary entry for February 20, 1823, d'Estréhan Papers, Historic New Orleans Collection.

72. Thouin, "*De la greffe des arbres,*" in *Dictionnaire d'Histoire Naturelle,* 2:134.

about 48 percent silica, 18 percent alumina, and 33 percent lime. The word was also sometimes used for heavy or clayey soil, for which there was a better name, *terre forte,* a mixed soil in which the dominate feature was clay. French nurserymen defined *terre de bruyère* as soil from the beds of forests "such as Chantilly or Fontainbleau," composed of thick leaf compost, but modern dictionaries define it as peat.[73] Chaptal defined black *terre de bruyère* as 39 percent sandy silica; 47 percent vegetable humus; 7 percent aluminum; and 6 percent carbonate of lime.[74] While Lelièvre used these terms without defining them, he also simplified the subject for his readers, dividing soils into three basic types: sandy (*la cilice, ou sable pur*), clayey (*l'argile, ou terre glaise*), and chalky (*la terre calcaire*).[75]

Lelièvre also presumed the reader's knowledge and use of the *serre* (greenhouse). One writer has credited the botanist Sebastien Vaillant with conceiving the use of this type of structure during the seventeenth century as a means of conserving coffee plants brought back to the *Jardin du Roi* in Paris from the Netherlands, to which they had come from India. Guy Crescent Fagon, director of the *Jardin,* immediately built "vast ventilated glass buildings heated by pipes" for the exotics coming in from around the world, and a new genre of building was launched.[76] By 1684, what had begun as a simple idea for a coffee plant had developed into the gigantic *orangerie* designed by Jules Hardouin-Mansart at Versailles, which today houses over a thousand potted orange trees, palms, and pomegranates during winter.[77]

Typically, the French soon developed the use of the *serre* into an art,

73. Oxford University Press, *Oxford Superlex: The Oxford Hachette Dictionary English-French* (Oxford, 1994–1996), s.v. *"terre de bruyère."*

74. *Dictionnaire d'Histoire Naturelle,* 1:lx–lxi.

75. *Nouveau Jardinier,* 25.

76. Duval, *King's Garden,* 35.

77. Pierre Lemoine, *Versailles in Color* (Versailles, 1981), 40.

dividing the main types into *serre chaud, serre froid, serre temperée, bâche,* and *orangerie* depending on the amount of effort required to keep the glass house warm in winter. Of these, the *serre temperée* and the *orangerie* were perhaps the most interesting. The former was a glass house in which the temperature was kept constant by means of inside hotbeds and a furnace manned throughout the night in winter. The wall sloped down on a forty-five-degree angle from a height of eleven feet in the rear to three feet in front. The *orangerie,* which looked less utilitarian and was frequently designed by an architect, was a tall house for wintering trees in which the ceiling was expected to be three to four feet above the highest branches. It was kept dry inside, which reduced the need for extra heating, and was sometimes dug out at the bottom.[78]

Lelièvre mentioned the *serre* in his book and used the verb *serrer* (to tighten or store), ignoring the fine distinctions that the French made among types. The *serre* may have been more important in Europe than it was in the mild Louisiana climate, but New Orleans gardeners were known to have them. For example George T. Dunbar, a Baltimore native, civil engineer, and railroad surveyor who completed several plans now in the Notarial Archives collection, had a greenhouse at his home on Common Street (now Tulane Avenue) during the 1840s. Dunbar maintained some two hundred camellia japonicas and other ornamental plants and garden structures in the greenhouse and on the grounds of the home, which has been the site of Hotel Dieu Hospital since soon after his death in 1851.[79]

Another interesting example of the *serre* in antebellum New Orleans was that of Louis de Feriet, a market gardener and rum distiller in the Faubourg Clouet about a mile and one-half downriver from the Vieux

78. Noisette, *Manuel complet du jardinier,* 89–100.

79. Jacob Soria, N.P., February 6, 1851; W. H. Peters, N.P., July 20, 1855; R. Brenan, N.P., February 2, 1853, NONA.

Carré. De Feriet, a French émigré and former baron from Metz in Lorraine, had settled in New Orleans in 1803 and two years later married Maria de la Merced St. Maxent, the daughter of a wealthy Creole. De Feriet's elaborate home and gardens, assembled on Dauphine Street between Louisa and Clouet over twenty years beginning about 1820, could have come right out of Lorraine. The property included a two-story *orangerie*-like greenhouse of generous forty- by eighty-foot dimensions, roofed partly with slate and partly with sash. It had a southern exposure, and its rear wall was adjacent to the stables, a good source for manure.[80] De Feriet also had a pecan orchard in the rear of his property, with trees arranged in rows. He grew oranges that, like d'Estréhan's, all died in the deep freeze of February 1823. De Feriet soon replanted the trees, which by June of that year were growing well, although they were probably very small. He added the greenhouse in a period of prosperity in 1835 to protect his plants both from cold and from what he called the "dog days" of summer. He enlarged it in 1837 and again the following year and built a small rail spur to transport his large potted orange, lemon, and guava trees inside,[81] just as the French did in Paris.

De Feriet's garden was partly ornamental and partly utilitarian. As a younger man just getting started in New Orleans, he had depended on the revenue from a farm in the *Métairie* where for some years he grew red beets, white radishes, white-headed York cabbage, long orange carrots, round turnips, currants, green peas, gooseberries, and other vegetables that Lelièvre would mention years later. De Feriet could sell such vegetables at the Washington Market, just a block from his home on Dauphine and Louisa. He also shipped barrels of pecans to New York

---

80. *Plan d'une Propriété Dans le 3.M Municipalité,* Plan Book 21, [Jacques] de Pouilly, May 8, 1847; A. Mazureau, N.P., December 8, 1842, NONA; de Feriet Papers, letters no. 3 (November 12, 1816) and no. 23 (January 20, 1821), Tulane University Special Collections MS B350.

81. De Feriet Papers, letter no. 178 (June 26, 1838).

and Havana. In the front of his Dauphine Street complex were two geo-metrically arranged parterres leading to a more romantic style serpentine garden. Among the plants in these ornamental sections were verbena, arborvitae, moss rose, dwarf banana trees grown from seed, and the "Mexican lily." "I often have visitors," he wrote to his sister in 1838, "ladies and gentlemen who admire my garden extravagantly, which has nothing very unusual in it, although they say it does."[82]

De Feriet's geometrically focused parterres were similar to the gar-dens of many New Orleanians at this time. As Charles F. Zimpel's monumental 1834 *Topographical Map of New Orleans and Environs* and a significant number of Notarial Archives drawings attest, New Orleans property owners had in large part absorbed from their eighteenth-century forbears the notion that the parterre in varying geometric shapes was the standard for gardens.[83] As a result, the question of garden design was something of a settled issue, more so than it was in other American cities and in the works of writers in English. This given was probably a prerequisite for Lelièvre's remark that although the length of his work did not permit him to cover all the developments in flower cultivation, once he had stated the general principals of this culture as clearly as possible, every person of intelligence would be able to "culti-vate his parterre." One gets an image from all this in some distinction from the appearance of old yards in New Orleans and environs as they emerged from the late nineteenth century. Many had, and still have, just one centrally placed walkway bordered by evergreens such as azalea,

82. Michel de Armas, N.P., November 24, 1819, NONA. The *Métairie* is a suburb of New Orleans in Jefferson Parish. For Washington Market, see Plan Book 102, f. 8, NONA. For discussion of plants grown, see de Feriet Papers, letters no. 3 (November 12, 1816); no. 26 (May 10, 1822); no. 30 (September 21, 1822); no. 178 (June 28, 1838).

83. Nineteenth-century archival drawings in NONA are full of garden design evi-dence. For a sampling see Turner and Meek, *Gardens of Louisiana,* 4–5. The Zimpel Map may be viewed at Tulane University Library, Southeastern Architectural Archive.

boxwood, or aspidistra. Grass occupies the sunny areas that were formerly parterres, and mature live oaks and magnolias overhang the rest. The *Nouveau Jardinier* is a standing testimonial to a different aesthetic.

The *Nouveau Jardinier de la Louisiane* was not to be Lelièvre's only venture in book publishing, although it is his only known composition. Like Boimare, and Jourdan before him, he continued to publish and promote local books, always in French, always to fill some pedagogic or intellectual need to promote both French education and the education of French-speaking people in New Orleans. In 1840 he published *Manuel des Verbes Français, Reguliers et Irreguliers,* by Louis Dufau. The next year he published *Précis Elémentaire de Géographie à L'Usage des Ecoles Américaines (Concise Elementary Geography for Use in American Schools)* by Dezanche, a New Orleans educator and tutor who had written the manuscript for his own use in teaching after finding it impossible to educate the children in his charge without an elemental geography in French. Lelièvre then published the manuscript because a number of teachers had applied to Dezanche for copies. Not surprisingly, the geography covered both America and Europe and featured a disproportionately long essay on Calvados, Lelièvre's home region. In it he reminisced about the "old seignuries," the "old university," the lace, the tile manufactories, the apple cider, the weavers, the horses, the cloth weavers, the seaside cliffs, and the Norman roots back to William the Conqueror.[84] That same year Lelièvre published Victor Debouchel's *Histoire de la Louisiane, Depuis Les Premières Découvertes Jusqu'au 1840.* This was written to fill the gap in the state's published history between the end of the War of 1812, when historian François-Xavier Martin had concluded his annals, and the world of the 1840s. Four years later, Lelièvre republished a French edition of an American history that a New Or-

84. Dezanche, *Précis Elémentaire de Géographie à L'Usage des Ecoles Américaines* (New Orleans, 1841), 1:199.

leans teacher, Madame Leiris, had translated from English.[85] In the meantime Lelièvre was ever seeking new business and new intellectual outlets, even developing an art school in 1841.[86]

A second marriage, to Olympe Mougneau of New Orleans, brought Lelièvre a new set of relatives and help with the bookstore. The second Madame Lelièvre would expand the business after his death and carry it forward for decades. Her sister Elizabeth Georgette Mougneau, a capable woman, ran the bookstore in the absence of her sister and brother-in-law on their business trips to Europe. On one of those trips in 1854 Lelièvre died at the age of fifty-nine in Bordeaux, having left Georgette Mougneau in complete charge in New Orleans, even to the extent of selling the business. She had not sold it; the subsequent estate inventory revealed that the bookstore of J.-F. Lelièvre at 210 Royal, corner St. Ann, was still in his estate, still stocked with some fifteen thousand books.[87]

Madame Lelièvre returned to New Orleans from Bordeaux and promptly went into business with her sister. The two styled themselves "Veuve O. Lelièvre & Co." for forty additional years. The sisters bought real estate, operated a hotel, expanded and enlarged the bookstore, and specialized heavily both in things French and in things Catholic. They prospered on the crest of Victorian religious sensibilities as New Orleans experienced it, selling thousands of holy cards, missals, plaster statues, gold crosses, saints' engravings, chaplets, rosaries, and veils. They sold vestments to the expanding archdiocese, offering a variety of chasubles, albs, chalices, pyxes, ciboria, gilded censers, monstrances, processional crosses, candlesticks, and candles in wax "*très*

85. Mme. Leiris, *L'Histoire des Etats-Unis, Racontée aux Enfans* . . . (Paris, 1835; reprint, New Orleans: J. F. Lelièvre, 1845).

86. Pitts and Clark, *City Directory for New Orleans* (New Orleans, 1842); *L'Abeille* (January 26, 1842), sec. 3, p. 17b.

87. A. Ducatel, N.P., March 15, 1854, NONA.

pure." They also catered heavily to the cemetery culture that was in full bloom in late nineteenth-century New Orleans. They met the demand for tomb ornaments made to order using all kinds of materials—pearls, velvet, dried flowers, pansy garlands, moss, and hair. They offered crêpe in white and black, by the yard or by the piece. They carried Baccarat crystal, Bohemian glass, and gilded candelabras. Customers could also find tea caddies, glove boxes, domino and lotto games, French and German toys, parasols, and perfumes "from the best houses of Paris." They opened a branch on Baronne Street near Canal, which they called *La Succursale,* the French word for a branch chapel operated by a church parish.[88] In this locale near the "downtown Jesuits" Church, a religious store survived in New Orleans until recent times.

The *Libraire Classique et Réligieuse* was still flourishing when Madame Olympe Lelièvre eventually sold her interest to her sister Georgette, by then the wife of James Porter. Madame Olympe then retired to the Haute-Pyrénées section of southern France, where she lived a comfortable life as a *rentier.* Her stepson, Eugene Nicolas Mougneau Lelièvre, oversaw business operations in New Orleans during the 1870s on behalf of the partnership.[89]

Not until 1880 did the family finally get title to the locale the business had occupied for eighty years, when the wardens of the cathedral finally sold the land they had controlled since the 1730s. The Lelièvre bookstore survived there until 1894. During the twentieth century the building it occupied was the home of Sherwood Anderson and his wife. The Andersons sold it to Elizabeth T. Werlein and her family; Mrs. Werlein is credited today as the chief instrument in the founding of the

88. *Almanach de J. F. Lelièvre Calculé Pour La Nouvelle-Orléans Pour L'Année 1871, et Après le 4 Juillet La 98.e de L'Independance Américaine* (New Orleans: J. F. Lelièvre, 1871). A copy of this rare book can be found in the Special Collections at Julane University's Howard-Tilton Memorial Library.

89. Theodore Guyol, N.P., December 11, 1872, NONA.

Vieux Carré Historic District and Commission. The building, reconstructed by the wardens of St. Louis Cathedral in 1834, still stands.[90]

Through writing, publishing, bookselling, and family life, Jacques-Felix Lelièvre took his place in the intellectual ferment that was New Orleans in its antebellum period. In the widest context, he was part of the movement that impelled thousands of middle-class Frenchmen to head for New Orleans in the aftermath of the French Revolution and Napoleonic Wars. Once there, each contributed in his or her own way to the spread of French ideas and the growth of French culture in the face of a veritable storm of competition from other cultures and ideas.

In a narrower sense, it seems Lelièvre stepped effortlessly into the world of French book selling in New Orleans, one that had been growing steadily since 1800. He held his own there for the rest of his relatively short life. The lives of his two wives bracketed his own career in New Orleans, one laying the groundwork for his activities and the other carrying on his name and his business for long years after his death.

In the world of horticultural writings, Lelièvre's book was both pathbreaking and sequential. It was the first of its genre in Louisiana, not a *flore Louisianais,* which had already been attempted,[91] but a manual to work with. It was the first and one of only two books on Louisiana gardening to be written in the nineteenth century—a time when horticultural writing was in ferment both in Europe and in America. And yet it was not cut from whole cloth. It drew on the spirit of eighteenth-century France and the writing of nineteenth-century France. It formed a bridge from the findings of the Abbé Rozier, André Chaptal, Duhamel

90. J. Cuvillier, N.P., July 22, 1847; J. F. Meunier, N.P., June 4, 1880, and July 2, 1894; F. D. Charbonnet, N.P., August 25, 1925; Sol Weiss, N.P., September 16, 1926, NONA.

91. Constantine Samuel Rafinesque, *Florula ludoviciana; or, A flora of the state of Louisiana. Tr., rev., and improved from the French of C. C. Robin, by C. S. Rafinesque* . . . (New York: C. Wiley, 1817).

du Monceau, Dumont de Courcet, Louis Noisette, André Thouin, and others to an American audience. It translated their philosophy by urging the gardener to acclimate new species and improve native ones by applying scientific methods of managing both plants and the environment. These practices would serve them to better advantage than gardening by the cubit, by rule of thumb. In the final analysis, if in mirroring early nineteenth-century French horticultural thinking the flavor of the *Nouveau Jardinier* seems more European than Old South, then perhaps it is well named.

The success of *Nouveau Jardinier de la Louisiane* is difficult to measure. Unlike the *New American Gardener,* it enjoyed only a single edition. Some eighteen copies have been identified in modern American research libraries, confirming the volume as a rarity. That a few volumes survive, however, is evidence that it was purchased and probably used. American horticultural writers of the nineteenth century evidently failed to refer to Lelièvre's work in their own publications, no doubt because it was in French. Thirty years after its appearance, however, St. John the Baptist Parish resident Ulger Vicknair published a slim volume intended to recommend methods and varieties adapted to warm weather to the French-speaking families who grew vegetables in this old Creole parish. Vicknair noted in his introduction that "other [vegetable manuals] have indeed been written for Louisiana, but by authors using theory without practice."[92] If he meant Lelièvre, this fault did not prevent Vicknair from plagiarizing the *Nouveau Jardinier de la Louisiane* in a number of entries.

Today horticulturists still doubt that cold-season annuals can be grown successfully in lower Louisiana for most of the year, and perhaps, in the end, the techniques of managing cold in Europe had greater promise for success than those of managing heat and humidity in Loui-

92. Vicknair, *Le Jardinier Economique,* 3.

siana. But the optimistic outlook on overcoming obstacles to growing that pervades the *Nouveau Jardinier de la Louisiane* is refreshing. The twentieth century has leaned heavily on mechanization to produce goods and in some cases has abandoned the belief that preindustrial methods have value. Here in the *Nouveau Jardinier de la Louisiane* one may rediscover for a moment the joy of a gardener facing Mother Nature with little more than a well-educated pruning knife and a hoe.

A Note on Methodology

Jacques-Felix Lelièvre evidently knew more about horticulture than about grammar. The French text of the *Nouveau Jardinier* is replete with paragraphs penned as single, multiline, run-on sentences with up to ten clauses or phrases connected by commas. While French (and English) writing styles of the day did tend toward long sentences, the error level found in Lelièvre's work was by no means typically French, nor does it appear in his sources. One can visualize Lelièvre composing his book by extracting the phrases or thoughts he wanted to use from his dense sources and then jotting them down in a series. For reasons that may range from ignorance to an assumption that his readers might prefer the staccato style, he published the book without polishing his sentences.

While it is ordinarily desirable to preserve the sentence structure of a copy text, Lelièvre's ubiquitous stylistic and grammatical errors tend to obscure his meaning and diminish the reader's enjoyment of an otherwise fascinating work. For these reasons, I have rendered a free translation, silently transposing commas into semicolons and providing conjunctions just before the final phrase of numerous sentences. In extreme cases I have also supplied periods, bringing the train to a full stop and beginning a new sentence. Another large emendation involves the somewhat tedious sections on astronomy, originally in the first chapter, which have been moved to an appendix.

The reader should also note that Lelièvre alphabetized his entries on vegetable and ornamental species by their French common names, and the translation maintains the original order of the entries though the headings have been translated into English. (See the index for help finding entries for individual plants. Though the index is based on Lelièvre's, items are alphabetized by the English translation of each term.) However, to give the reader as much information as possible, the French common names as the author originally offered them (which would ordinarily have been omitted) and the Latin botanical names are also provided, in brackets.

Since Lelièvre did not offer botanical names, we might have encountered difficult terrain trying to provide translations into two other languages if it had not been for his consistent plagiarism from the *Bon Jardinier*. The *Bon Jardinier* proved to be the Rosetta stone of the *Nouveau Jardinier* translation. With this book in hand, I was able to move from the French common names and plant descriptions in the *Nouveau Jardinier* to the frequently identical or almost-identical language in the plant lists of the *Bon Jardinier*. From the *Bon Jardinier* I extracted the botanical names, checked them in Bailey and Bailey's *Hortus Second* to corroborate the botanical and English common names, and ultimately came to firm ground after a tortuous journey. In the presentation, we thus offer the English common name, followed by the French name, followed by the Latin name.

Market garden in Faubourg Marigny, 1840.
Courtesy of New Orleans Notarial Archives.

One will always find in the shop in Lelièvre's Bookstore a large assortment of *FRENCH AND AMERICAN SEEDS.* He carries all kinds of fruit Trees and ornamental plants.

His contacts with the best Nurserymen of France and of the North permit him to be sure that his orders will be filled and with all possible speed.

━┈◆┈○┈◆┈━

J. F. Lelièvre's Bookstore is always full of educational, devotional, and literary Books; Office Furnishings, Supplies for drawing, fancy goods, and Children's Toys.

Subscription Library.

NOUVEAU
JARDINIER
DE LA LOUISIANE,

CONTENANT LES INSTRUCTIONS NECESSAIRES
Aux Personnes qui s'occupent de Jardinage.

PAR J. F. LELIEVRE,

Ex-Jardinier-Agriculteur du Gouvernement Français
pour les Colonies.

NOUVELLE-ORLEANS.

CHEZ J. F. LELIEVRE, LIBRAIRE,
Encoignure Royale et Ste.-Anne.

1838.

NEW LOUISIANA
GARDENER

‹›—‹›—○—‹›—‹›

✦ INTRODUCTION ✦

My aim, in composing this work, is not to teach a course in agriculture. That material has been treated by skilled growers so as not to leave anything to be desired. However, in addition to their treatises being too long for use in ordinary gardening and too voluminous for ease of use by most people interested in it, they have also the trouble of being written for climates from which the one here differs by the intensity of the heat and the movement of the sap in relation to the seasons.

A work especially adapted to the needs of the region was therefore needed by those who, deprived of the knowledge necessary to a gardener, want to direct the works in their gardens themselves, which is why I determined to compose this book.

The methods that I describe are in part the fruit of my experience; the ideas I lacked were obligingly supplied by growers experienced in this country.

I have spoken of some plants little or not at all used in Louisiana, but which might be cultivated here with success, the richness of the soil permitting all expectations when the plants entrusted to it are managed according to wisely combined principles of cultivation.

The limits of this work being too compact to provide a full development in the individual article that the cultivation of each plant requires, which would moreover produce too frequent repetitions, I have combined at the beginning of the work the preliminary knowledge indispensable to everyone who wishes to garden. I thus call the attention of my readers to the instructions [the sections "Soils" through "Crop Rotation"], in which the fundamental principles of agriculture are laid out.

I felt that fruit trees merit particular attention. It is surprising that these precious plants would have been neglected up to this moment in Lower Louisiana. If the attempts that have been made up to now have not had the success one might expect from them, that can be attributed only to a lack of perseverance or to not using the proper means to assure their success. I have described as clearly as possible how to handle them from the time of planting to their complete maturity; I note here that the preparation of the holes in which they are to be planted is one of the most essential things, the too great moisture of the soil appearing to me to be the principal obstacle to overcome. I insist on the acclimation of [new] species by grafting [them] onto wild species that grow in the woods, or by collecting pollen from their [wild species'] fruits. Several attempts repeated with appropriate care either in cultivation or in finding the most favorable exposure for various species will lead, I have no doubt, to satisfactory results.

There is no need to reject a plant when it does not succeed during the first years of its introduction to a [particular] climate. One must realize fully that culture more or less modifies the nature of vegetation, and that, through well understood care, one can succeed in naturalizing plants to which the climate once seemed completely adverse.

Flowers form the last part of this work; all those to which I apply nomenclature are easy to cultivate; and so a garden enthusiast will, with the assistance of the procedures that I indicate, be able to cultivate the plants of hot climates; it will suffice for him to provide them a level of heat corresponding to that of the countries to which they were native; to keep them, during the winter, in a well-lighted place; and to guard that moisture does not bother them, taking care to clean them by brushing them lightly each time he notices a white substance forming on any part whatsoever of the plant.

The method that I propose to destroy coco vine may appear erroneous to many people who think it is indestructible. Some of them, in fact, will pretend to have used the procedure that I recommend without success; but if they had persisted and applied all the care that I recommend, I am persuaded that their land would be purged. I am even more convinced of it, [because] since I wrote this article, several growers have assured me that they had success with it, using similar means. Let everyone be persuaded then that what is necessary is work *at the opportune time* and the perseverance to make this noxious plant disappear.

This work will perhaps not respond to all of the readers' needs, but it will suffice, I hope, to bring noticeable improvement in the cultivation of useful plants. Those who wish to have more extended instructions may consult more complete treatises; they are great in number.*

*Among these works one may choose: *The Farming Botanist,* by Dumont de Courcet; *The Course on Cultivation,* by A. Thouin; *The New Course of Agriculture,* by the members of the Agriculture Section of the French Institute; *The Gardener's Manual; The Gardening Almanac; Complete Course in Agriculture,* by Abbé Rozier.

NEW LOUISIANA
GARDENER

⊱┄┄⊙┄┄⊰

SOILS

Soils are divided into three large classes by agriculturists; these are: silica, or pure sand; clay, or loamy soil; and calcareous soil.[1]

Earth composed entirely of one of these kinds of soils, without a mix, will be essentially sterile. Fertility depends on the happy combination of at least two kinds of these soils. It is difficult to judge the quality of a field from the color of the ground; however, experience proves that black and friable soil is the best, when this color is not owing to an excessive amount of decomposed carbon. There are some very fertile red soils; but generally white soils are hardly productive, because lime or clay dominates in them.

The soil of Lower Louisiana, on the borders of the Mississippi and between the lakes, is generally silico-clay, that is to say, composed of sand combined with clay; across the lakes the soil is siliceous. This difference of nature requires some modifications in cultivation.

The environs of New Orleans are low and marshy, which makes the cultivation of vegetables difficult.

WATER

Water is a powerful agent for vegetation. It is this which draws up the nutritive juices and serves as a vehicle to transmit them to all parts of the plant, but it becomes harmful when excessive; it is thus necessary to try to control it.

All the growers in this country understand perfectly the system of improving the land; all have little drainage canals, or ditches, which cross their plantations in every direction. These methods suffice for the cultivation of cane and corn, but they need some perfecting for the cultivation of vegetables.

He who would cultivate a little garden with a spade should, after dividing his ground into squares, dig some deep ditches around each one.

These ditches, covered with planks, will serve as paths for circulation in the garden, and the soil that comes out of them, thrown back on the ground, will help to elevate it. Each square will be divided into rows three or four feet wide, according to the kind of plants that will be grown there.

The rows will be separated by a little walkway, on the sides of which one digs a shallow trench which will facilitate the flow of rainwater toward the ditches; the rows must be convex, that is to say, more elevated in the middle than on the sides. The ditches should communicate with the improvement canals and carry the extra water out of the garden.

In large-scale cultivation, the existing ditches and canals must be maintained and cleansed so as to avoid stagnant waters. The rows tilled by plow should all end at one of these ditches, their midpoint elevated, the sides flattened and separated by a deep and well-excavated furrow; the more the soil is low and moist, the less wide the rows should be, and, in this case, those that do not exceed the width of sweet potato mounds would be preferable because the water, running off with greater facility, will harm the plants far less.

To suitably round the rows, it is necessary, in plowing them, to back them twice over. To back means to lap the two first furrows one over the other in turning the plow to the right at each end of the field; to split open again is to open the row by turning the plow to the left; in this manner there remains an open furrow in the middle of the row. At the first plowing the earth is broken; the furrows are lapped in the second, and so on, alternately. Since it is essential that all parts of the ground be well worked, the second time one turns it over, first of all open a furrow in the middle of the row, with two passes of the plow, that is to say, after having first opened a furrow (I call a furrow the trench opened by the plowshare of the plow), return to the same one so that the amount of soil is nearly equal on each side. Plowing then in the opposite direction, one will throw this soil on the turned-over earth, which will conveniently form convex ridges. I observe that once this elevation of the turned-over soil is obtained, it will be easy to maintain it without the help of a double turning; this preparation is necessary only at the time of the first plowing.

DROUGHT

If too much moisture harms vegetation by rotting plants or weakening them, drought is not less harmful. This is why it is necessary, as much as possible, to remain vigilant against these two extremes.

In small gardens one combats drought by irrigation, and to that effect one must dig several wells in different parts of the garden, to have a sufficient quantity of water to bring to all the plants. Sprinkling systems are assembled with buckets of tin or copper, called *watering cans.*

The pipe through which the water flows has a perforated spout from the end of which the water falls like rain. One should water all the seedbeds with the spout; and for very delicate seeds a spout pierced with very fine holes is needed, so that the water, falling a little bit at a time, will moisten the soil without beating it down. A spout pierced with holes too large will produce a harmful effect, because of the crust that results from it. The soil hardens, and germination is arrested or the seed rots. When watering plants newly transplanted, and strong enough to stand a generous watering, remove the spout, and place a straw stopper in the pipe so as to allow a thumb-wide stream of water to flow; water around the base of the plant, to compress the soil near the roots, which makes it root again more easily; but after the soil has soaked up the water, take care to throw a little bit of dry soil or sand in the little basin that has formed, to prevent a crust from forming. This precaution must not ever be neglected each time one repeats the watering in this way, unless one at first creates a little basin around the plant and fills it with compost, chopped straw, sawdust, or some other material that will suffice to lessen the effects of water and drought. Under this cover the soil will remain cooler, and will not harden. However, an inconvenience may result; if one fills the basin with fermentable materials, the fermentation beginning in the materials may draw rot to the base of the plant; it is necessary therefore to take care to leave an inch uncovered around the stem, when covering with dung, horse manure, or any other like thing.

Watering being practically impossible in large-scale cultivation, one must search for the best means of reducing the disastrous effects of a prolonged drought as much as possible; these means consist in plowing and hoeing, about which I will speak further on.

AIR

If air is necessary to man, it is not less necessary to vegetation. The breathing of plants through their pores is no longer in doubt; also, everyone recognizes that the air exerts a great influence on them. Hardy plants, for the most part, tolerate variations in the atmosphere fairly well; however, when they are young, especially after transplanting, one must protect them from air that is too hot and, above all, from the broiling rays of the summer sun, by appropriate coverings; give them free air movement during the night so that they may enjoy the salutary influence of the coolness and the dew. Coverings placed over the plants at nine or ten o'clock in the morning, must be removed in the evening at sunset, and that just until the plants have rooted again, if they have been transplanted, or until they have enough strength to resist the sun, if one is covering seedlings. These coverings must be arranged so as not to interfere entirely with the circulation of the air, and composed of straw matting extended on cross pieces supported by forked pickets. However, when one is transplanting in an open field of a certain size, this procedure is not practicable; then one contents oneself with inserting in the ground, near the base of the plant, a leaf of any kind, big enough to shade the plant entirely, and supported in the middle by a small stake. This work, very easy, may be performed by children. The leaves so placed over the plants, will fall over like an umbrella, and protect them sufficiently to have them take root, but one must take care to remove them as soon as they are no longer useful, because then they will harm the plants which, under this covering, will send up shoots too tender to resist the rays of the sun.

HEAT

Heat is also one of the chief agents of vegetation, when it is accompanied by a certain degree of moisture. Air too hot and dry dries out the plants and entirely destroys the moisture of the roots, if one does not take care to water frequently; cold joined with moisture weakens plants and promotes the multiplication of insects, which often kill them; too great cold restricts the sap and prevents the plants from flourishing. It is therefore necessary to consider the state of the atmosphere when one wants to sow, plant or graft. Southern and southwestern breezes are the most favorable, because they always contain some humidity; the west wind is almost always cold and wet, that of the north always brings a dry cold; the east wind has a burning quality which injures plants a lot, particularly trees in flower.

Left to themselves during a rigorous winter, plants are affected differently by cold, according to their nature or the climate where they originated; some persist, although without growing, during the most severe freezes, others perish at the least cold; one also sees others which deteriorate more or less as the temperature decreases. Cold is not very destructive to large-scale cultivation, because care is taken to adapt the sowing to the season, and not to risk tender plants to the time of severe cold. However, when one wants to have the first fruits of the season, one must have recourse to artificial means to produce the heat indispensable to the development of plants. For plants from warm climates there are greenhouses, but for vegetables one contents oneself with hotbeds, shelving beds, and cold frames.

HOTBEDS AND SHELVING BEDS

Hotbeds are squares made of new manure; that of horses is the best.

Build a mound of dung four feet high by an equal width. The exterior sides of the bed must be well tied together, and the manure well tucked up in each bed that one lays, without which it will collapse and the fruit of the work will be lost.

Cover the pile of manure with one layer of compost (manure well rotted and reduced to soil) eight or nine inches thick. Let the bed so prepared lie for eight days to allow the excessive heat which radiates from the manure to escape, then one may sow or plant without fear; before this time the fermentation which begins would make the seed moldy and rot it. After some time the manure loses its heat, and the plants will suffer if the bed is not reheated; reheat it by putting some new manure all around in a thickness of two feet, and on the whole top of the bed. When one has several beds in a row one after the other, reheating is accomplished by filling the space between them with manure, which must be not less than three feet. When this manure cools, it must be removed and replaced by more; in this manner one can maintain the degree of heat that one wants in the bed.

To concentrate the heat further, cover the plants with glass domes or with sash. To install the sash on a bed, one must have a wooden frame, higher on the north side than on the south, so that the rain can run easily over the glass and fall outside of the bed: the sash must be fixed on hinges on the front; use notched props to raise the rear of the sash when you want to give the plants some air, which need not be done except from ten in the morning until two in the afternoon. When the heat of the sun is too great, cover the domes or sash with straw mats or palm leaves.

The most favorable arrangement of the beds is to align them from east to west, the north side or rear a little bit more elevated than the south side or front, so that the surface faces the sun the more.

Vegetables grown in hotbeds, which grow rapidly, may be replaced frequently; these ordinarily are lettuce and radishes, when one wants to have them all year round. Seeds of first melons and cucumbers are also planted in hotbeds, along with cauliflowers, *beringènes,* tomatoes, and all the seeds that must be transplanted and of which one wants to advance the time of production. Ordinarily, one also plants flower seeds in hotbeds to have the plants ready earlier for transplanting. There are also hotbeds for mushrooms, of which I will speak later, when I treat the particular cultivation of each plant.

Several vegetables, such as green peas, green beans, and kidney beans may do without hotbeds, for early varieties, but one must shelter them from cold with shelving beds.

These are a kind of windbreak or artificial wall aligned in an east-to-west direction. Lay out a well-cultivated and suitably manured bed on the south side of this wall and there plant seeds of green peas, beans, etc., which, being protected from the north wind, will produce their fruit much earlier than in the open air. If a frost is feared during the night, have straw matting to set up against the wall, so as to protect the plants. It would also be good to cover in time of cold rains.

Those who in the summertime want to raise lettuce, radishes, etc., which ordinarily cannot stand up to intense heat, can erect a lath house in the open, made of stakes set up on both sides, on which rest cross-pieces which support a light covering, either of straw (large mats) or of palmetto leaves. This shade house should be at least eight feet high, so as not to impede the free circulation of air. It would be good to arrange the covering so as to allow it to be removed during rains, which, forming gutters across the covering, will fall like a jet on the plants and uproot them. It would also be good to uncover during the night so that the plants may enjoy the dew and the fresh air, which will hasten their development.

PLOWING AND HOEING

Earth too compacted will easily crack, and all gardeners know how harmful these cracks are to plants. Those that are near the crevices will suffer first, then die for lack of nourishment, because the air being introduced to a great depth will dry out the ground which, in this condition, will not supply the roots the nourishing juices necessary for growth. Plowing and hoeing at the right time will partially prevent these accidents.

Plowing must tend to break up and lighten the earth. In a small garden, it is in breaking up the clods well, spading extensively, and then in passing the steel rake, that one lightens the soil; but to obtain these results in large-scale cultivation, one must begin by lightly skimming the ground with the plow, removing only a light, two-inch layer. If the weather is wet, one must wait until it has dried a little bit to pass the harrow, but if it is dry one must harrow right away; this light layer will break up easily, because the clods, having only a little thickness, will give way to the stroke of the harrow and fall apart without trouble. After several days give a second plowing by removing a layer two inches thicker, which is harrowed like the first; a third plowing will attain a depth of six to eight inches, and the soil will be well broken up if the weather has been favorable and if it has been well harrowed each time. One must not sow or plant until the fourth plowing, and in that last dressing the plow should not go deeper than at the third, but only lightly grate the bottom, so as not to bring clods to the surface.

Earth so prepared will retain its freshness for a long time, and if one can cover it with a half inch of manure or sawdust, one will not have to fear cracks. However, since one does not always have sawdust or manure at his disposal, it is necessary to supplement by hoeing.

When a hard rain falls on well-broken soil, the surface hardens, and at the first sun it forms a crust which will progressively grow if it is not broken. In gardens a raking given to the beds will suffice to break the crust and arrest the progress of dryness, and the seeds placed in the ground, experiencing no obstacle to their development, will grow vigorously; while when they are compacted under a hard, thick crust at the surface, they spend themselves in vain efforts to pierce it, and most often perish without seeing the light of day.

In large-scale cultivation the rake is too costly and time consuming; but one can supplement it with a very light harrow which is passed once or twice on each side of the furrow, if the seeds still have not sprouted, because then the harrow will bruise the root of the plant, destroying it.

On plantations the ground must be lightly pricked with a small mattock called a hoe or fork hoe. This instrument generally has two teeth on the side opposite to the cutting edge; these are used for hoeing plants that one fears cutting in half, such as carrots, turnips, salsify, etc. Cabbages, lettuce, and everything that is transplanted into rows may be hoed with the cutting edge or with the fork hoe. One must always hoe in dry weather. This operation is not only advantageous [to prepare] for rainy weather, but must also be repeated as often as possible: because, in addition to breaking up the soil, which, having recompacted, will obstruct the growth of plants, it tends also to reheat soil too cold, by allowing the air to penetrate it.*

These precautions may appear meticulous to some gardeners accustomed to abandoning their plants once they have confined them to the earth; but if they would think about the few fruits that they harvest from their cultivation, their [own] interest will lead them to try methods that promise them greater abundance.

What I have just said relates only to heavy soils. I should also indicate what ought to be done with sandy soils, or soils in which sand dominates.

These soils being dry by nature, and very susceptible to air, one must be sparing with the plow. A good dressing that mixes the soil well will

---

*It prevents cracks in soils that are too heavy, and serves to destroy weeds which, growing more quickly than plants, obstruct them, weaken them, and kill them if one does not remove them.

suffice ordinarily, but one should avoid giving it more than two. Hoeing ought also to be less frequent, and be done only to destroy weeds that obstruct [the growth of] vegetables; it ought always be shallow, performed with the scraper and not the pickax.

During dry periods, sand retains humidity fairly well, provided that one contents himself with lightly skimming the surface when hoeing. These sorts of soils are improved by mixing them with mud, cow manure, and all kinds of cooled manure soil, whereas one must use plaster, lime, and horse, sheep, chicken, and pigeon dung for cold soils.[2]

HARMFUL PLANTS

All soils contain greater or lesser amounts of harmful vegetation, which it is important for the gardener to destroy. Many kinds come simply from the seed dispersed throughout the soil, either by the wind or from straw that contained seeds the preceding year; sometimes these seeds are also carried by manures, birds, the feet of animals in wet weather, etc.; these kinds of weeds are easy to destroy, a single hoeing ordinarily sufficing. But plants with perennial running roots are often more tenacious; there are even some that are regarded as indestructible; it is with those that we must contend more particularly.

The bitter coco has for long years been the despair of growers in Lower Louisiana; it appears that all the methods used up to this day to destroy it have been fruitless. I know some gardeners, however, who have become master of it, and I believe that with work and perseverance we will come to destroy it completely. Not in spreading lime, soot, or other materials on the soil will we succeed, but by natural methods, those indicated by true principles of cultivation. Here is what I propose: when a field is infested with coco, plow it carefully, in order to break up the soil well. If the root is abundant enough to be piled up in a heap, put the fire to it; in this manner one will relieve oneself of a large part; but if one cannot use this method, one must spy out the moment when the coco has sprouted and is well out of the ground, [and] give a shallow plowing, but cut all of the stems precisely; this operation, repeated during a summer, every time the coco appears, will weaken the plant, and one will perceive in the fall that it will already be diminished a great deal. One must combat it above all during the month of May, because that is the moment when the sap is in full ascent. Two or three plowings well harrowed to bring the root above the ground will well advance its destruction. During the winter the coco does not grow; the soil may be covered with winter plants that will be harvested before its springtime sprouting.

In the spring, begin again to oppose it at its first appearance, by plowing frequently, from March to the end of May, and at this time, the soil being well broken, sow in the field a plant that covers the ground well, that grows quickly, and that remains standing until autumn; the coco, choked by this plant, will not reappear, or, if it sprouts, it will be weakened and so feeble that a light plowing after harvest will suffice to complete its destruction. If, in spite of this work of two years, it reappears again in the third, do not be disconcerted, but on the contrary redouble your ardor, multiply your plowing or hoeing, above all during the month of May, taking care to harrow upon each plowing, to pull the roots out of the ground, and I am convinced that after this third trial, the land will be perfectly cleaned out.

The preceding that I indicated is deduced from well-recognized principles of agriculture, that in wearing down the plant one kills it.

Pruning a plant stimulates it to sprout; each time this operation is repeated, it is obliged to make new efforts to put out new stems, and when these efforts are repeated often, the expenditure of sap is so large that it cannot be offset by the absorption of nourishment; the plant withers and dies. The most vigorous tree, if all of its branches are cut off a certain distance from the trunk, will put out afterwards vigorous shoots that will become more handsome than the first, but if one cuts these shoots again when they are five or six inches long, and repeats this operation without ceasing, before the end of the year the tree will be exhausted and will die.

The same cause will produce the same result in all species of plants.

I have advised sowing during the second year, in earth that one wants to purge of coco, plants that are capable of smothering it; the one I believe is the most appropriate for this use is the buckwheat (black wheat), of which the numerous branches covered with large leaves, fill in and form a tissue so thick that no plant can grow under it. Different kinds of vetches or field cabbages sown thickly can replace the buckwheat, but vetches, having frail stems, become enfeebled too easily, lie over on the ground, and are often covered by the plants one wants to destroy.

Too much rain and strong wind can also knock buckwheat down, although it resists ordinary kinds of bad weather fairly well; it should be sown in May or June. Mow it when the seeds on the lower branches are fully black; arranged under a beehive covering it will ripen its other seeds and dry; shell it in the field; the straw makes good fodder, and may be fed to animals, above all to cows, who seek it out when it is fresh; the seed serves to fatten poultry; and a flour known in America as *Buckwheat* is made from it.

INSECTS

Numerous insects attack plants, some under the ground and others above it. The cricket or mole cricket is a small insect nearly the same shape as the domestic cricket; it causes much damage in seedbeds, by excavating an underground tunnel like the mole. One often sees seed-beds dug up in every direction by this insect, the result of which is always the loss of a large part of the young plant. Often-repeated experience has proved that the best means of destroying them is to pour oil in the holes. However, since it would take a long time to find the holes one by one, one would sooner mix a small quantity of oil in the irrigation water. This mixture can be made in the watering can, by putting a good size glass of any kind of oil in each bucket of water. Ants are repelled in the same manner; but since these insects are much more numerous than moles, one must first drench the part one wants to purge with oily water, then each day give a light watering with the same kind of water.

Slugs sometimes do a lot of damage to young lettuce plants, cabbage, radish, etc. Seedbeds are protected from them by spreading, in the evening, on the ground, powdered quick lime. Soot can also be used. A cordon of lime or soot, surrounding a seedbed on all sides and without gaps, will prevent slugs from the area from entering.

Caterpillars are destroyed by dousing plants with water in which black soap is dissolved, in a quantity sufficient to make lather by stirring with the hand; but it is always necessary to sprinkle very early in the morning, because as soon as the sun appears the caterpillars hide under leaves, and will not be touched by the soap water, unless one takes the precaution of hitting the undersides of the leaves, which would take a long time.

To protect a seedling from being cut in two by little insects that attack plants at the moment of germination, it is necessary to prepare the seed before planting it, as follows: for three pounds of any seed whatever, mix well an ounce of flowers of sulfur; put all of it in a well-sealed bottle; twenty-four hours later add another ounce of flowers of sulfur, and mix; stop up the bottle again; after twenty-four hours, mix another ounce of flowers of sulfur, so doing for the following four days; the fifth day, plant the seed, which will have acquired a smell so strong as to repel insects until the young plant is well emerged from the earth.

The flowers of sulfur can also be dusted over the seedbeds; the odor it gives off in sunshine repels insects. One can also lime the seeds; to do that slake some quicklime in an amount of water sufficient to moisten the seed that one wants to plant; when the lime is well slaked and almost cold, pour it over the seed which is stirred until it has absorbed all of the lime-saturated water, let it dry, and the next day plant it. To do this correctly, the seed must be covered entirely while drying with a thin layer of lime.

RATS AND MICE

Some vomic nut, grated and mixed into a patty of meat, or with some cheese, poisons rats and mice; but it is necessary to prevent domestic animals from getting near it. Those who regard this method as dangerous, may, independently of snares, mouse traps, etc., get some deep vases, more narrow at the opening than at the bottom; by sinking them in the ground just up to the level of the earth, and keeping some water in them up to 6 inches from the top of the vases, an unlimited number of little four-legged creatures will fall into it and drown. A proven method for rats, and in use in several seaports in Europe, is to catch two rats alive, enclose them together in a jar, without giving them any food for three days; the fourth, throw them a living rat, the two prisoners will fall upon it and devour it. Continue giving them a living rat to devour for several days, taking care to let them fast long enough each time for hunger to press them, and free them at the end of eight or ten days; these two rats will eat only their like and will destroy a great number. One can so procure several pair of destructive rats; but it can become dangerous to multiply them too much.

FERTILIZERS

Fertilizers serve to reestablish in the soil the nutrients worn out by too active vegetation. They must always be suited to the nature of the soil. Rubbish that contains a lot of alkalis is a very good enrichment for moist soil, because of the absorbent quality of the old plasters of which it is composed. After rubbish, choose, for cold soil, the hottest manures, such as that of horses, pigeon droppings, sheep dung, etc. It is necessary, for this sort of earth, that they not be too well composted; if they are made of long straw, they will break up the soil better.

On the contrary, dry soils, and particularly sand, require cold fertilizers; cow or pig manure, the mire of seaweed and canal dredging, [and] street mire suit them because, in addition to their containing a lot of humus, they serve to link up the overly fragmented parts of the soil.

Several growers wanted to quantify the amount of manure necessary to fertilize a field; for large-scale cultivation of grain and hay, this is possible, but in general it is a bit difficult to determine this quantity. For gardening, one does not ever have to fear adding too much; one can cover the ground with two or three inches, without danger, before plowing, and with one inch after sowing or planting. There are, however, several plants that are not adapted to newly manured soil. I will be sure to indicate these.

CROP ROTATION

The substitution of different plants grown on the same land is called rotation. It is recognized that if the same vegetable is planted in the same place several times in succession, production will diminish after several years to the point of becoming null; but if crops are suitably alternated so that the same plant is not found on the same land except after three or four years, and, if enrichments are a matter of course, the soil will not wear out, and one will always have abundant harvests.

There can be no fixed rule for rotation; it is up to the knowledge of the gardener to judge by the plants that he has put in his ground which ones should succeed them in that place. One should not, for example, plant parsnips or beets after carrots, because these root crops are so similar in their mode of growth that the land would become fatigued the second time; instead one would sow peas or beans, lettuce, cabbage, etc.; [and] over these onions, leeks, etc., in laying out his land and his seedbeds so that three or four years pass without the same plant reappearing in the same place. In general, one should not sow a taproot plant upon another taproot plant, nor succeed two runner plants twice, but alternate. A taproot plant, such as the long beet, would be replaced by cabbage, cabbage by peas or beans, beans by carrots or salsify, these by onions, etc.

The scope of this work does not permit me to inform my readers any further about the general principles of agriculture. What has come before, if well understood, will suffice for intelligent people who want to cultivate their gardens themselves. At this time I shall pass on to the Gardener's Almanac, in order to focus afterwards on the particular culture of the most utilized plants in this area.

GARDENER'S
ALMANAC

➤━┤━◆━┤━◯━┤◆━┤━◅

✧ JANUARY ✧

Sow in well-prepared soil: green peas, early green beans, radish and
long radish, lettuce, endive, celery, short carrots, early white-headed
Bonneuil cabbage, Alsace cabbage, English cauliflower, tender cauliflower, broccoli, melons, and early cucumbers, in hotbeds; eggplant, tomatoes, anemone paws, ranunculus claws, and flowering bulbs, and all
early plants in hotbeds or in full sun to be transplanted into place as
soon as the plant is strong enough. Cover the young plants at night, for
fear of frost; water at noon if the weather is dry.

✧ FEBRUARY ✧

One may repeat the sowing of January. In addition: turnips, short
and long carrots, parsnips, salsify, black salsify, onions, leeks, scallions,
kidney beans, parsley, escarole, cabbages—sugarloaf, York, St. Denis,
[and] Battersea; plant garlic and shallots, potatoes, Jerusalem artichokes,
asparagus, all kinds of seeds of trees and shrubs; plant dahlias, fruit and
ornamental trees; sow strawberries, all summer flowers in hotbeds; poppies and corn poppies in flower beds and in large clumps; orange and
lemon pips; make cuttings of all kinds of shrubs. At the end of the
month, prune trellised peach and apricot trees, apricots in the open,
plum trees, [and] grape vines. Remove dead and unneeded wood from

trees in the open; cut back* raspberry and gooseberry plants to make them sprout new wood. It is in this month and the following that one does cleft grafting.

✦ MARCH ✦

Seeds planted in February are repeated in March, either to replace the missing plant, or to succeed it. Mountain spinach, sorrel, carrots, parsnips, turnips, salsify, black salsify,[3] onions, spinach, chervil, cress, nasturtiums, purslane, all kinds of lettuce, chicory, escarole, cardoon, and beets may still be sown; sow in the open ground: asparagus, peas, beans, butter beans. This is the time to plant pimento and all summer vegetables.

Separate and transplant artichoke offshoots; plant asparagus paws, sweet potatoes, sorrel for propagation; thyme, lavender, rosemary, etc. Finish pruning fruit trees.

✦ APRIL ✦

During this month all of the seeds of the preceding month may be sown. This is the time to sow pumpkins, gourds, squash, and all cucurbitaceous plants; corn, oats, and the small seeds named in March; all annuals. Plant tuberoses, Spanish pinks, poets' pinks, julienne pinks, etc. Resow seeds of plants that failed; transplant the young plant that is vigorous enough. Plow unkempt ground during dry weather, that is to say, [ground] full of weeds.

✦ MAY ✦

Beets may still be planted during this month, as well as all of the root crops that one could not plant earlier. Beans of every variety in the open

---

*This means to cut the plant back to the point where the branches sprout.

ground, green peas (in the shade), dianthus seeds, wallflowers, etc. It is still the time to transplant artichoke eyes.

Pinch back pruned trees, grape vines; flute and crown graft. If you have sweet potato vines big enough, replant them in the open ground.

✤ JUNE ✦

The heat being already very great, one must not plant any more except in the shade, except for which the seedlings would be overheated.

Plant winter cabbage for transplanting in August. Those who would use the methods I have indicated, can obtain during summer: lettuces, radish, peas, beans, chervil, spinach, etc., of which they will harvest a good part, considering the scarceness of these vegetables in summer.

✤ JULY ✦

During this month the heat is too strong to sow in the open ground; only in the shade can one sow carrots, parsnips, or onions, to be transplanted in September. Toward the end of the month sow cauliflower, broccoli, and all the varieties of cabbage that one has not yet planted. Plant lily offshoots, mountain lily, and all the bulbous plants that must not be stored out of the ground.

Graft shield buds at a sprouting eye: cherry trees, apricots, peaches, prunes, apples, pears, etc. Layer pinks and all the plants one wants to propagate this way.

✤ AUGUST ✦

Although the heat be very great in this month, one must sow several seeds that will not succeed very well at other times, such as York cabbage, sugarloaf cabbage, white-head cabbage, [and the] cabbages of

Bonneuil, Alsace, [and] Milan; winter lettuce, sorrel, parsley, chervil, red and white onions, all to be transplanted in October; turnips for fall, scallions, etc. Plant anemones, jonquils, and hyacinths. One can still graft shield buds of cherry trees, wild cherry trees, old peach trees, and almond trees.

✤ SEPTEMBER ✦

The seedbeds that one may have neglected to build during the preceding month must be made at the beginning of this one. Plant strawberries to enjoy in spring; sow black radish, carrots, parsnips, turnips, and all the root crops that one plants in spring, taking care to cover (as in June, July and August) while the sun is shining, and water frequently. Sow early peas, Dutch beans, and bunch beans. All kinds of lettuce, chervil, parsley, rampion, wild rocket, etc. At the end of the month, graft shield buds at dormant eyes.

✤ OCTOBER ✦

Sow lamb's lettuce, spinach, lettuce, radish and long radish, [and] cauliflower, to be transplanted after cold weather. Plant eyes of artichoke, which will produce in spring, hyacinths, narcissus, jonquils, anemones, ranunculus, etc. Sever dianthus layers, [and] put them in pots to store in the greenhouse during cold weather.

✤ NOVEMBER ✦

This is the month when one must concern oneself with hotbeds, because with cold weather approaching, the attentive gardener must be on guard against its bad effects. One sows asparagus with greater success this month than in the spring. One can risk lettuce in the open ground, [along with] radish and long radish; if cold snaps come late, one can enjoy them. Do not neglect to sow spinach during fall and winter, because, not tending to bolt in these two seasons, it can be cut several times; the same is true with all immature vegetables subject to bolting. If the sap has fallen, it is time to prune apple and pear trees; pull up and replant those one wants to replace; but this operation must never be done when the trees are in sap.

⇥ DECEMBER ⇤

This month and that of January are the coldest of the year, which is why one must not plant seeds except in beds and under cover; for large-scale cultivation one should engage only in the preparation of the land that one wants to sow in the spring, watching not to plow except in dry weather. If it freezes, one must plow without harrowing; the ground remains more open, the air penetrates more, the freeze cuts it; but then it is not necessary to harrow except after a good thaw [when] the clods will fall to pieces under the teeth of the harrow; this is the best means of breaking up the earth.

The grower of first fruits must redouble his zeal; the hotbeds and their reheating must be cared for with energy and discernment; this is the moment to make nature work by all artificial means possible.

The planting of trees which has not been possible before this period must be accomplished. One can even prolong this operation until March; it will succeed, provided that trees uprooted for a long time have not put out too strong shoots, which will have exhausted the sap. At this time, during dry weather, one must clean out drainage ditches and ready the earth to be covered with growth in the spring.

THE CULTIVATION
OF PLANTS MOST USED
IN LOUISIANA

>·◂▸·O·◂▸·◂

GARLIC

·‑·▦▸▦·‑·

[Fr. *Ail;* Lat. *Allium sativum* L.] Garlic is propagated by seed or by pods; the month of March is the most appropriate time to plant it. But if seed is sown, one must take care not to pull up the bulbs before the second year. Garlic is harvested when its leaves have dried up.

PEANUTS

·‑·▦▸▦·‑·

[Fr. *Arachide;* Lat. *Arachis hypogaea* L.] This plant, originally from Central America, can acclimate itself to temperate regions.

As soon as cold weather has passed, plant in little pots two seeds in each, sink the pots in a hotbed, and raise the plant in this manner until it is strong enough to be transplanted. Toward the end of May, when cold weather is no longer to be feared, take your plant out of the pot and plant it in a single clump into well-cultivated and fertilized soil; soon the plant will flower and will make little pods which it will bury in the ground to ripen.

In addition to the fruit of the peanut being agreeable to eat grilled or in candy, a very good oil is extracted from it, which may substitute for olive oil.

GOOSEFOOT (BEAUTIFUL LADY)

[Fr. *Arroche;* Lat. *Atriplex hortensis* L.] Sow in February or March, September and October; all kinds of ground suit it; water if the ground is dry. The leaves of this plant serve to sweeten sorrel, whether in soup or in stuffings; they are also used in gumbo z'herbes.

ARTICHOKES

[Fr. *Artichauts;* Lat. *Cynara scolymus* L.] Artichokes grow in clumps, formed from numerous shoots which come from the root and which we call offsets. The offsets serve to renew the plant; this method is quicker than planting the seed. It also has the advantage of always reproducing the same kind, while the seed is subject to variations.

Separate the offsets of old artichoke feet from February to April, so that the plant will bear fruit in fall; the offsets replanted in September will bear the following spring. This plant lives three years.

Divide the square that you want to plant into rows three feet wide, with a one-foot-wide footpath. In the middle, plant the artichokes three feet apart; some gardeners plant them in clumps formed from three eyes planted in a triangle six inches on each side. This method is perhaps the best, because if one or two feet fail, the planting is not bare.

Artichokes do not like cold; they are protected from freezes by mounding them up in winter and by covering them with stable litter, dry leaves, or heads of cane. The young plant wants to be watered frequently; deeply worked ground is necessary.

The seed of this plant is sown at the end of April or the beginning of May, in substantial and well-cultivated soil; place the seeds three inches apart and one inch deep. Transplant the plant in place when it has acquired enough strength to sustain this operation.

ASPARAGUS

[Fr. *Asperge;* Lat. *Asparagus officinalis* L.] In spring, dig ditches three feet deep, by an indefinite length; make a bed of two feet composed of material suitable to absorb moisture, such as rubbish, plaster, even carbon, pieces of brick, or oyster shells; throw in haphazardly, so that the moisture flows across; put a foot of earth over this, then four inches of humus; plant the asparagus paws in two rows twenty inches apart, and cover them with three inches of humus (or well-improved soil). Weed, hoe during the summer; in the fall put three more inches of soil on top; in the spring, give it a little working; during the summer, hoe again, weed, water in dry weather. The following autumn cover the asparagus with manure, leave them resting so during the winter; in mid-February, throw another three inches of soil over the manure. When the asparagus sprout, if the stems are fat and vigorous, cut the nicest ones without waiting another year. In general, they should not be cut until the end of three years.

The third year, in winter, uncover the asparagus and remove three inches of soil which is thrown on the footpaths; put an equal amount of manure in its place, replace the soil in the month of January or February, so that there are six inches of soil on top during the winter and nine during the summer.

In the month of October, or as soon as the seed matures, cut the stems, work the ground, uncover, and replace some manure. Each summer one must weed, hoe, and water, repeating the same care each year.

To get beautiful asparagus, one must not cut them except at the end of three years, when paws have been planted; if one sows seed, it is necessary to replant the young two-year paws, and wait the same amount of time after this transplanting as for the paws separated from old stock.

For the first asparagus of the season, one must plant old paws in hotbeds and under sash, in November; they are covered with two inches of soil and six inches of good new and warm manure. At the end of eight or ten days remove the manure, but replace it with the same thickness of humus; set up reheating layers around the beds; at the end of fifteen days the asparagus will appear and will produce an abundant harvest for one month. By planting anew each month in a new bed, one will have asparagus continually during the winter; one must cover when one expects a too severe cold.

EGGPLANT

[Fr. *Aubergines (brehêmes)*; Lat. *Solanum melongena* L.] I have already indicated the season when this vegetable must be sown in the hotbed. The season can be advanced still more, if one wants to force early fruits, by sowing in pots filled with good humus; sink them in a good new hotbed, and under glass; when this bed has lost its warmth transfer them into another, and, continuing so, one can obtain fruit at a time when its value will amply compensate for the costs incurred. When one has sown this plant in a bed and it has gained enough strength to be transplanted, one must transplant the plant in rows four feet apart while leaving a three-foot interval between each plant in the row.

As this plant does not produce much shade, one can retain part of the ground by sowing below it some seed that will not bother it, such as parsley, chervil, [or] radish; or even plant lettuce there.

BEETS

[Fr. *Bettterave;* Lat. *Beta vulgaris* L.] The normal season for the sprouting of the seed of this plant is the month of March, which is also the most favorable time to sow it. One may, however, advance or delay if the season obliges. Sow at a distance of 8 to 10 inches between each seed. Take care to stamp or press down the earth in order to compress the seed, because being full of bumps, it will not very soon receive the amount of moisture necessary for its development without this precaution.

One may continue to sow beets from the end of July until October, to have them in spring. They must be covered when it freezes.

BREDES OR FALSE SPINACH

[Fr. *Brèdes* or *faux epinards;* Lat. ?] This plant may appear too unimportant to attract the attention of growers; however, it is somewhat well used in this country, where one species grows spontaneously, which makes its cultivation very easy. It is found in all soils of Louisiana. Its branchy stalk, armed with thorns and garnished with leaves similar to those of the amaranth to which it is congenerous, grows to two or three feet. Its leaves which, in the natural state, have a disagreeable taste, are used in gumbo z'herbes. They can take on a sweeter taste through cultivation, and replace spinach with some advantage, for which a thornless variety is already substituted in several countries.

By sowing the seed mixed with that of foxtail amaranth, one could obtain several varieties, of which one will in the end merit attention and serve to garnish our tables with a delicious and thoroughly creole dish.

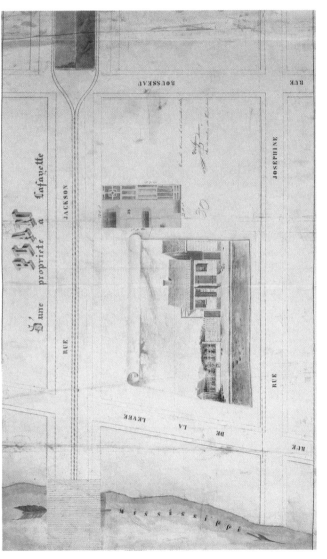

Plan of a property in the Lafayette community of old New Orleans. "Voilquin architecte," December 15, 1843. Creole cottage (*ca.* 1820) on Jackson Avenue near Tchoupitoulas, with parterre, arbor, and rows for vegetables. Property sold by Estelle Drouet Engelle to Hannah Martin McIlvain in 1844. (Plan Book 21, folio 6) *Except where noted otherwise, illustrations in this section are courtesy of the New Orleans Notarial Archives (hereinafter cited as NONA).*

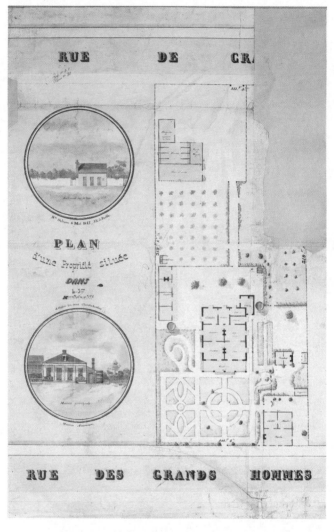

Plan of a property in the Third Municipality. J. N. de Pouilly, May 8, 1847.
Louis de Feriet home and gardens on Dauphine Street in Faubourg Clouet, built
in the 1830s and featuring geometric and serpentine parterres, pecan and orange
orchards, and a greenhouse. (Plan Book 21, folio 31, NONA)

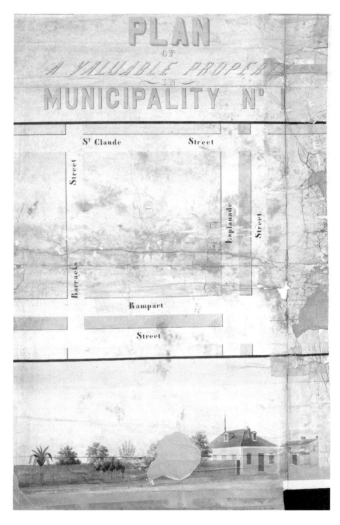

Plan of a valuable property in Municipality No. 1. Claude Giroux and Alexander Castaing, *ca.* 1851. Creole cottage at Rampart Street and Esplanade Avenue with luxurious garden in the style of the 1830s, arranged in a double parterre with orbital central features and crosswalks. The garden became part of the Joseph François Avet property in 1868 and was maintained well into the twentieth century. (Plan Book 28, folio 44, NONA)

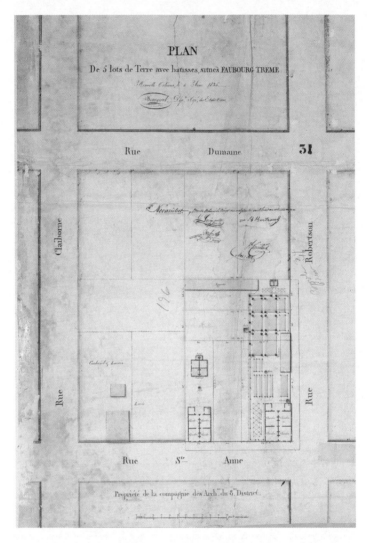

Plan of five lots with buildings in Faubourg Tremé. Jean Antoine Bourgerol, August 6, 1835. Market garden at St. Ann and Robertson Streets in Faubourg Tremé, with beds laid out in both rows and squares and, like many New Orleans market gardens of the period, ornamental features, including two arbors. (Plan Book 34, folio 46, NONA)

Plan of five lots in Faubourg Marigny, Fifth Municipality. **Em. Allou d'Hémecourt, July 22, 1840.** A shrubbery-filled, walled garden, becoming overgrown by the time of this drawing, adjacent to a small Creole cottage. Horace Broadman Rose, who built the house and probably installed the garden, had sold the property to Philippe Guesnon in 1832. (Plan Book 37, folio 29, NONA)

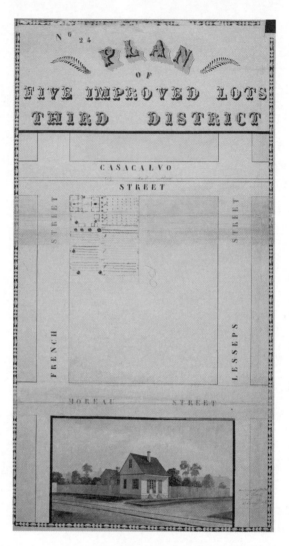

Plan of five improved lots in the Third District. Adrien Persac, August 28, 1866. A fenced market garden with beds in long rows and perhaps a fruit orchard, probably cultivated by Adam Nuber since the 1840s, at Casa Calvo (Royal) and France Streets, downriver from the Vieux Carré. (Plan Book 38, folio 23, NONA)

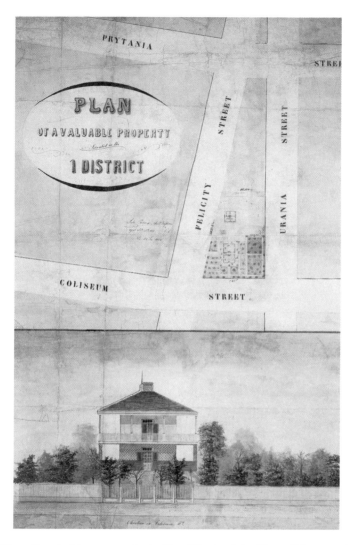

Plan of a valuable property in the First District. Jules Ricou, February 28, 1858. A brick house surrounded by galleries and a lush garden on Coliseum Street in the Lower Garden District. The property was developed by William Smith in the 1830s and sold to Jacques Arthur Guillotte in 1838. (Plan Book 42, folio 28, NONA)

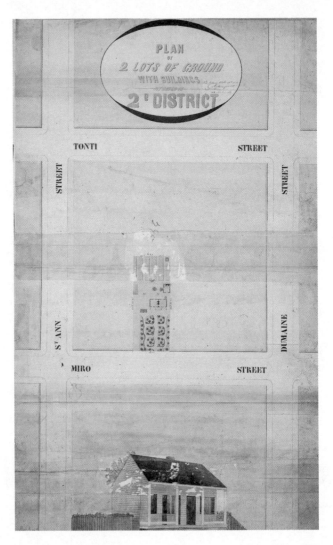

Plan of two lots with buildings in the Second District. Alexander Castaing, October 12, 1858. A modest, two-room galleried cottage with both ornamental and vegetable beds, the irregular outlines of the parterre showing a creative approach to a traditional form. (Plan Book 45, folio 49, NONA)

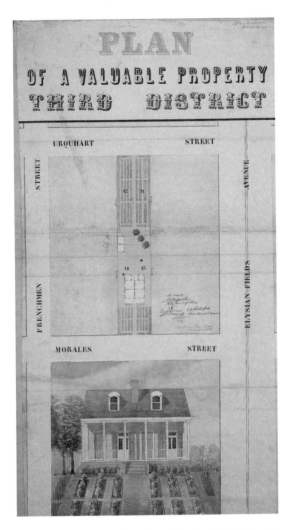

Plan of a valuable property in the Third District. F. Nicholas Tourné and Charles G. de l'Isle, June 7, 1858. Creole cottage residence of florist Antonio Ferdinand Lemos, in the bricks-between-posts style of the 1830s, with sixty-square-foot gardens, trellises, and, in the rear, numerous fruit trees and grapevines, advertised in 1858 as "one of the most beautiful parterres in the city, enclosing a large variety of rare plants, and shrubs." (Plan Book 48, folio 64, NONA)

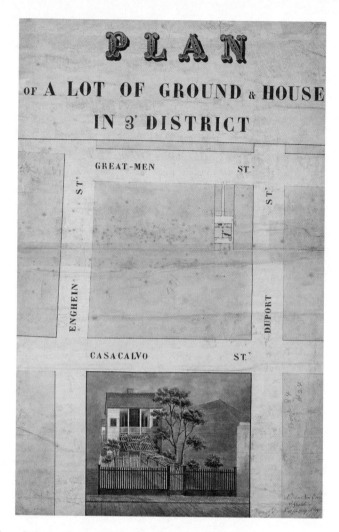

Plan of a lot and house in the Third District. Pietro Gualdi, January 7, 1855.
An unusual house set well back from Great-Men (Dauphine) Street, as if a
dependency remnant from some lost structure, with an arbor in front and a
second courtyard, or *basse cour,* in the rear, a peculiarity of many lots in French
Creole neighborhoods. (Plan Book 84, folio 24, NONA)

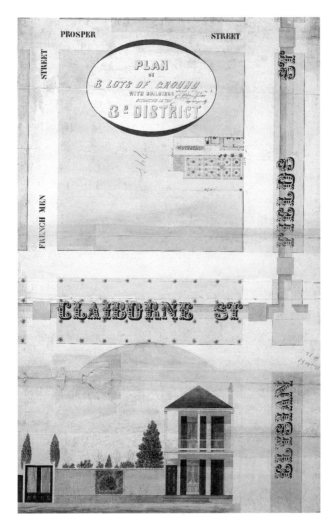

Plan of three lots with buildings in the Third District. Alexander Castaing, February 17, 1860. A two-story house in the style of the 1840s with a formal, French-style garden, featuring numerous sections and intersecting walkways, the suggestion of a pedestal near the front, and a *potager* in the rear. The house belonged to François Gras, a French-born candy maker, who had purchased it from Joseph Girod. (Plan Book 89, folio 12, NONA)

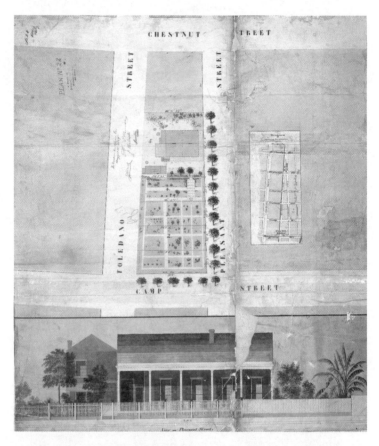

[Title unknown.] **Ludwig Reizenstein, July 31, 1867.** A house and garden dating to the 1830s, on a lot carved from the Dalassize Plantation. Despite intact vegetable squares and arbor, the drawing shows the garden has not been maintained, with trees matured in the beds, only a few scattered plants, a flowering banana spilling over the fence, and street trees lining the property. In its day, this garden may have supplied the public market at Magazine and Harmony Streets. John McGovern built the house, which had a series of owners, including Matthew Ryan, Mary L. Caldwell, and Bernard Kendig. (Plan Book 103, folio 18, NONA)

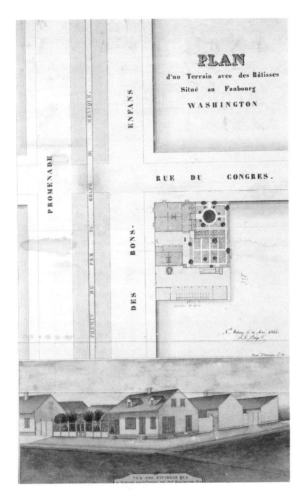

Plan of a lot with buildings in Faubourg Washington. J. A. Pueyo, March 14, 1844. Property developed in 1838 at Congress and Bons Enfans (St. Claude) Streets, with parterre, two arbors, and vegetable beds; large *four,* or oval oven, and stables in rear were used for baking and delivering bread and vegetables to neighboring markets. Paul Trumpf built the house and probably installed the garden. Louis Barthelmey Rey and Mrs. Victorie Lecesne, free persons of color, purchased the property and sold it to Marie and Josephine Colmare, also free persons of color. (Plan Book 6, folio 100, NONA)

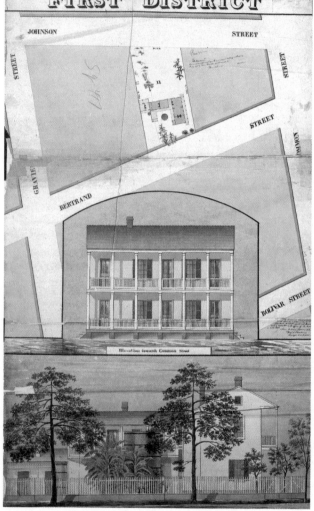

PLAN

OF

A LOT OF GROUND

ATED IN THE

FIRST DISTRICT

JOHNSON

STREET

STREET

STREET

STREET

GRAVIE

BERTRAND

BOLIVAR STREET

Elevation towards Common Street

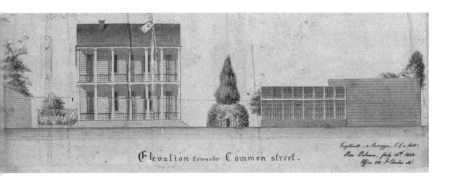

Opposite: **Plan of a lot in the First District. "Hedin and Schlarbaum,"** September 20, 1854. *This page:* **Plan of seventeen lots in the First District (detail). "DePouilly and Blanchard" and "Engelhardt and Nemegyei,"** 1852. Two drawings illustrating the home and garden of New Orleans surveyor George Towers Dunbar, facing what is now Gravier Street on the site of the city's former Hotel Dieu Hospital. The extensive grounds featured a greenhouse, hotbeds, an igloolike gazebo, and two hundred camellia japonicas. (Plan Book 64, folio 16, and Plan Book 13, folio 1, NONA)

CHOU TRÈS HÂTIF
D'.ÉTAMPES

CHOU DE BRUNSWICK A PIED COURT

BERNARD CARANT / PARIS

Detail of cabbage from *l'Album Vilmorin*. Established in 1775 and still operating today, the Vilmorin family's nursery in Paris was one of the sources from which Lelièvre would have ordered seeds. The nursery began publishing catalogs such as *l'Album Vilmorin* in the mid-nineteenth century; foremost among the illustrators was Elisa Chapin, to whom this drawing may tentatively be attributed. (From the personal collection of the translator.)

CARROTS

[Fr. *Carotes;* Lat. *Daucus carotta* L.] Same culture and same care as for beets, except that one sows more thickly.

To plant short carrots for an early crop, one needs a well-manured and frequently watered soil. Carrots may be transplanted. When the seedbed is planted too thickly, it is thinned by pulling up the plants that are too numerous, after having first generously watered the ground. These little carrots are thinned to three or four inches apart; so thinned, they will become less long, but fatter than those not thinned.

CELERY

[Fr. *Celeri;* Lat. *Apium graveolens* L.] Celery can be sown in any season, but during the winter it demands much care because of the cold. This plant loves in its youth a loose and rich soil. One would do well to sow it in the hotbed. Replant it into well-worked beds, and, when you want to blanch it, mound it up with earth or cover it with straw. Well-whitened celery ought to be preferred to other kinds, because it is more tender, and perhaps because it is more fashionable than the pink. Hollow celery ought to be rejected.

CHERVIL

[Fr. *Cerfeuil;* Lat. *Scandix cerefolium* L.] This is sown in any season; but that sown during autumn can be cut several times, while the seedlings of spring and summer will provide only one harvest, because it goes quickly to seed.

During the summer sow in the shade, or cover during intense heat.

MUSHROOMS

[Fr. *Champignon;* Lat. *Agaricus edulis* L.] This plant is as dangerous as sought after. Some species only are edible; the others are poisonous.

In winter it can be grown in the open, but during the summer it must be cultivated in a cellar if one does not want to risk the loss of the harvest, because a storm—a thunderbolt—can destroy an entire bed. The beds are made by digging a trench two feet wide by one foot or more deep; fill the trench or ditch about six inches with plaster, pieces of brick or shells, make a bed as indicated [above in the section on hot-beds], add six inches of horse manure to the top, and top the bed with the soil from the trench. Tread the bed well, and lay it out like a *dos de bahut,* cover that with an inch of soil mixed with sand or humus. After some time, cover[4] the bed with thick stable litter. You will see some white appear at first, then some mushrooms; do not let them grow too big, without, however, cutting them too small; they must be developed well enough so that the leaves underneath are well formed, and that they are fully white and free of black powder.

Grown in this manner, mushrooms make a delicate dish and one less unhealthful than those that grow in the fields and in the woods; all [of those] are indigestible, and many acquire poisonous qualities from the condition of the ground that supports them.

Good mushrooms are recognized by their completely white or pink color; the poisonous ones are either black or a very dirty white. When one sees spots or rotted parts on them, one should reject them. But since those with the best appearance may contain harmful ingredients, it is always prudent to be assured of their quality. The apparently surest method consists in boiling them with a silver coin; if the coin darkens, it is an evident proof that the mushrooms are poisonous; but they can be eaten with confidence if the coin maintains its original color.

ENDIVE

[Fr. *Chicorée blanche* or *frisée;* Lat. *Cichorium endivia crispa* L.] Endive is planted in beds in February and March, and in well-cultivated open ground, during the other months up until October; transplant when the plant is strong enough, into rows eight or ten inches apart; and water when the weather is dry. To blanch it, cover it with moss, in dry weather, while carefully gathering all of the leaves together. In this circumstance it is not necessary to water very much, because the water that stays inside the plant will rot it.

CABBAGE

[Fr. *Chou;* Lat. *Brassica oleracea* L.] Several species of cabbages are cultivated: the York cabbage and early Battersea are sown first; for a first crop, the small York should be preferred, growing very quickly and taking up little space. One can raise it in hotbeds during the winter, by protecting it from freezes, or transplanting it into the open ground in March, to head in May. This cabbage has a very good quality; a distance of ten inches suffices between each base.

The St. Denis and Bonneuil are called summer cabbages, because they produce in this season, although sown as early as the others. Winter, or late cabbages, are the Dutch, Alsatian, German, late Battersea, Drumhead, Glazed, and Quintal. All of these species can be sown from March until October, but the months of August and September are the most favorable. When the plant has attained a height of 4 or 5 inches, transplant as in a nursery, that is, into beds separated by 5 or 6 inches, leaving 3 to 4 inches of space between each cabbage. This operation is made with a planter, by sinking the cabbage up to the neck; one must always take this precaution when transplanting cabbage. Summer cabbages must be planted 18 inches apart, winter cabbages from 24 to 36 inches; the transplanting of these latter in place is done in November, December or January, if they are sown in autumn; or in May, if they are sown in the spring. Before transplanting cabbages, take care to cut the taproot to force the plant to make hair roots; also cut the galls or growths found on the root; this gall always contains a canker, which lives at the expense of the cabbage and slows or diminishes its growth. When cabbages are not transplanted into nurseries, they must be sown very thinly, so that they do not get feeble and the neck can gain strength.

Milanese cabbage, neglected in this country, could nevertheless be grown here advantageously; it is a curly cabbage, heading very solidly and of medium size. It resists intemperate weather better than do the other cabbages. It tolerates the sun and is not averse to a freeze which, instead of destroying its quality, makes it better, in slowing it and lending to it a green taste particular to it. One can sow it in May [and] transplant it in June; it will head in September or October, and will survive all winter in the ground. When frosts are severe, cover it with turf, and leave it in the ground.

Cavalier cabbage would be still more useful on plantations where milk cows are tended. This cabbage never heads, but it produces a very great abundance of leaves; ordinary freezes do not arrest its growth. One can sow it in May, transplant it in June, at least three feet apart; leave it to itself during the summer. When the growth becomes thin cut the basal leaves; the cabbage will soar upwards, sprout vigorously, multiply its leaves, and grow up to eight feet high. This forage is nourishing and greatly increases the milk of cows. After a frost, it makes excellent vegetarian soup, and its spring shoots make the best broccoli after those of the Malta.

CAULIFLOWER

[Fr. *Chou-fleur;* Lat. *Brassica botrytis* Desf.] If this excellent vegetable is more difficult to cultivate than the other cabbages, it makes up for it quite well by the quality of its production. Many growers consider it impossible to get good cauliflower in Lower Louisiana; however, the success obtained by some gardeners is bound to make believers [of others] when, by using the same methods, they will obtain the same results.

This plant does not require particular care except when it is small; once in place, it requires only ordinary hoeing. From the beginning of February to the end of April, sow in hotbeds and water frequently. As soon as the plant has doubled its leaves, transplant it into another hotbed, taking care to cover it to protect it from cold during the night [and] from storms and heat during the day; do not uncover except in good weather. For an early crop, transplant in place in a good exposure, against a backboard; in May one can put it in the open ground. Give light waterings in the hotbed; sprinkle once or twice in place if the weather is dry; cultivate often; and repel caterpillars and green flies. Cauliflowers produce from July to August. For winter and spring produce, sow in hotbeds of a moderate heat in August and September. Water frequently and cover because of the sun; put into nursery beds in well-improved and -cultivated soil; thin in place when the plant has attained enough strength; water and cover each base with a large melon, cabbage, okra,[5] or other leaf, supported by a small stake so that the cover does not sag over the plant. The effect of this cover is to prevent a too hot sun from scorching the plant before it is picked, the leaf decaying by itself, or one can remove it as soon as there is nothing more to fear for the plant. These cabbages will produce in winter and spring, according to the species and the time of sowing. It must be noted that this cabbage is quite averse to frosts; it must be covered during the winter. Cauliflowers demand new ground, well broken, and well manured.

BROCCOLI

[Fr. *Chou brocoli;* Lat. *Brassica botrytis cymosa*] Less difficult than cauliflower, it does not differ in cultivation except for the little bit less care given to it.

SCALLIONS/GREEN ONIONS

[Fr. *Ciboule;* Lat. *Allium fistulosum* L.] This plant can be sown once a fortnight from February until October, taking care to water in dry weather, and to shade during intense heat. Scallions are ordinarily transplanted. Lay out beds three and one-half feet wide [and] transplant the scallions into six rows while separating each plant by about four inches; in this manner they will benefit much, sending out offsets which form very fat clumps that entirely fill the beds.

CHIVES

[Fr. *Ciboulettes;* Lat. *Allium schoenoprasum* L.] These are small perennial green onions that are propagated by dividing the root, which is bulbous, and which one separates in February, March, September, or October. They are also propagated by seeds, which are rare.

Chives are ordinarily planted in borders, where they create a pleasing effect from their foliage, sustain the soil, and produce a bountiful harvest without harming other plants in the row or flower bed. They must be cut frequently if one wants them always tender.

GOURDS, PUMPKINS, OR SQUASH

[Fr. *Citrouilles, potiron,* or *giraumon;* Lat. *Cucurbita, Cucurbita pepo* L.] These plants, which are all varieties of the same species, are cultivated the same.

From the month of February until April, dig in substantial and well-prepared ground some holes about one foot and a half in diameter, by a depth of 8 to 9 inches. Fill these holes with manure up to the level of the ground, cover the manure with 6 inches of compost, surround the holes with the earth taken out of them to hold in the compost material; after several days, when the manure has lost its maximum heat, sow two seeds in each hole by planting them only one inch deep; water frequently. One can sow watermelon the same way to have an early crop; they can be advanced a lot if covered with glass domes.

Gourds and pumpkins can also be obtained by planting them in the open ground, without preparation other than for plants in general; but the fruit will be less abundant and above all not as sizable. In Europe, where they are careful with this plant, it is not rare to see pumpkins the diameter of a barrel. Several attempts with the methods that I suggest will convince one that an equal size can be obtained in this country. The holes should be 10 to 12 feet apart, because this plant runs a lot.

CUCUMBER

[Fr. *Concombre;* Lat. *Cucumis sativus* L.] This is cultivated the same, but it must be sown in hotbeds, if one wants to have the earliest crop. Several kinds of cucumbers are grown: the large white and the yellow, which are eaten in salads or stuffed; the long green, for gherkins; the serpentine cucumber; and the round prickly cucumber; this last one makes very good ragouts. Sweet gherkins are also made from it, as also from the long green and the serpentine.

For large-scale cultivation, sow in April or May, in the open field; they need only to be weeded well and occasionally watered.

GARDEN CRESS

[Fr. *Cresson alénois;* Lat. *Lepidium sativum* L.] One must sow once a fortnight, if one does not want this to fail, [for] this plant goes to seed easily. In summer, sow in the shade and water frequently. This cress will succeed in winter if protected from freezes; in this season it will have the same advantage as all the small seeds that do not go to seed in winter, and will survive longer; but if one wants it tender it must be cut young, because it promptly toughens. It shares the same properties as the watercress.

WATERCRESS

[Fr. *Cresson de fontaine;* Lat. *Sisymbrium nasturtium* L.] This plant requires a lot of moisture. It is sown along the borders of running streams, of fountains, or of some body of water that does not get stagnant. If one lacks a stream or fountain, one can sow it in tubs with a hole made near the bottom; stop this hole with a plug. Fill the tubs (which need only be 6 to 7 inches high) with 3 to 4 inches of soil; saturate the soil and throw in the seed. When the plant has come up, take care to maintain an inch of water above the soil; the cress will grow there as if by a fountain. Take care to change the water, by removing the plug from the hole to let the water in the tub flow out, and pouring in new water with care so as not to disturb the soil and wash out the roots of the cress, which would suffer from it. One can lay a small board on the soil in the middle of the tub; when gently pouring out the water, it will spread over the whole surface without shocking and without harming the plant in any way. Once the change of water is completed, remove the board.

SHALLOTS

[Fr. *Echalote;* Lat. *Allium ascalonicum* L.] In February or March divide the shallot bulbs and replant them in good soil. They are harvested as soon as the leaf dries.

SPINACH

[Fr. *Epinards;* Lat. *Spinaccia oleracea* L.] One can have spinach all year through multiple sowings. Those sown in August, in beds, will pass the winter and may be cut several times, but those sown in spring and during the summer will produce only one harvest, because they go to seed very quickly. This plant wants heavy soil, well worked, and some shade during the summer; in winter it grows in any exposure, but will succeed better toward the south than toward the north.

KIDNEY BEANS

[Fr. *Fève de marais;* Lat. *Faba major* H.P.] Plant in February under cover; in March and April in the open ground, in rows in the garden, or scattered in the field. To make the beans produce copiously, one must, when flowering begins, pinch back the head; that is, pinch the tip of the plant between the fingers; finding its growth arrested, it will direct its sap to the fruit which will ripen better and faster, [and] become more beautiful and abundant.

BROAD BEANS/POLE BEANS

[Fr. *Fèves plattes;* Lat. ?] The whole world knows this vegetable, justly valued in this country, because of the savory taste and abundance of its fruit, as well as the lovely shade that it produces when one lets it run over arbors. One can cover a wall with it, [or] a partition that one wants to hide. The flexibility of its branches lends itself to all needs; however, the vertical direction suits it the best. It is sown in rows in February and March, and in beds of three rows, putting the beans 6 inches apart from each other, or in pockets; make a hole with the hoe and throw 3 or 4 seeds in it. The pockets or holes should be at least 2 feet apart.

To get first fruits, sow in February, near a shelving wall, give it some stakes 4 or 5 feet high only, and cut the plant back to the level of the stakes, when it has gotten that high. The flowers of the lower parts will appear and will promptly ripen their fruit. Left to its natural growth in good earth, this plant will attain more than fifteen feet in height; it is thus necessary to proportion the stake [positions] to this height. Sown later, it tolerates open ground well. It is not resistant to cold.

STRAWBERRIES

[Fr. *Fraisier;* Lat. *Fragaria* L.] This plant, sought for the excellence of its fruit, is propagated by seed sown in the spring in the shade, and by shoots or young plants coming from sprigs thinned out in the spring or fall; it needs a loose, substantial soil without fertilizer; do not bury the seeds; give frequent light waterings; and if you want to have fruit each month, cut the [side] sprouts back as soon as they appear. Several kinds of strawberries are known; the cultivation is almost the same for all. Pineapple strawberry[6] is ordinarily planted in borders, where, more exposed, it produces to advantage, and its fruit is of better quality than in beds.

BEANS

[Fr. *Haricot;* Lat. *Phaseolus* L.] This plant is cultivated like the pole bean, modifying the distance between sowings, according to the height of the different varieties. One would imagine that the dwarf bean, which grows to only two feet, should be sown more thickly than the bean of Soissons, which grows to twelve. One must always proportion the intervals to the height of the plant, and arrange the sowing so as to promote the circulation of air.

When planting in rows, leave a large walkway and a reasonable interval between the rows, to facilitate hoeing; if planting in pockets, separate sufficiently, for the same reason, and also so that air can circulate easily among the clumps because, without air there will be no yield; the plant will wither and the flowers fail.

One must never neglect to stake those that require it. To do so is easy: when they are sown in pockets, set up three stakes, straight or angled into a triangle, around each pocket, or insert them deep into the ground so that the wind does not turn them over, and pull the tops together just until they touch; the beans in growing around them, will tie them together, and form pyramids of very solid growth. Beans growing in beds are staked by driving poles into the ground in two rows, against the outer row of each side of the bed, one or one and one-half feet apart from each other, and by slightly bending the tops of the stakes toward the inside. This arrangement will facilitate the circulation of the air by widening the walkway. Be careful to train the first shoots onto the stakes, and to push back inside those which tend to grow over onto the neighboring bed, which will obstruct the walkway. Dwarf beans are sown two and one-half or three feet apart between the pockets; one must double the distance for the staked kinds, which grow up to 5 or 6 feet, and for other kinds proportionally.

LETTUCE

[Fr. *Laitue;* Lat. *Lactuca sativa* L.] Several species of lettuce are cultivated, of which all are very tender and averse to freezes and too much moisture. For an early crop, sow all winter in hotbeds, under glass domes or under sash. These plants like a friable and light soil, covered over with compost. For lettuce in the open ground, plant in spring, after the frosts have passed, under cover, and thin as soon as the plant has 5 or 6 leaves; water in dry weather, weed and cultivate often. These plants must be kept in the shade during the summer, under a shade house, or at least covered with straw matting. With care, and by renewing the seedbeds every fortnight, one can have lettuce all summer.

LENTILS

[Fr. *Lentille;* Lat. *Ervum lens* L.] This vegetable is little grown in this country; however, it might be grown successfully in the sandy soils on the other side of the lake. Lentils need light and thin soil; a too rich soil will make them produce too much green growth, and only a small yield. They are sown thinly, in rows, at the same time as green peas.

Lentils are not eaten green; they are allowed to ripen on the bush; when the lower pods begin to open, the whole thing is mowed, left to dry on the ground, and then beaten with a flail to obtain the seed. The straw makes excellent forage, because of the little pods which, cut before their maturity, are not stripped off and remain clinging to the stem.

CORN SALAD/LAMB'S LETTUCE

[Fr. *Mâche;* Lat. *Valeriana locusta* L.] A small plant that is eaten in salads. The seed is sown in autumn, in well-enriched soil, at the base of a wall or in the open ground; it needs to be watered.

MELONS

[Fr. *Melon;* Lat. *Cucumis melo*] For the first melons of the season, sow in January or February, in hotbeds, under sash. Cut back the superfluous stem when the melon begins to run, monitor the flowering, and to have beautiful fruit, cut the branches a little bit above the ripened fruit, allowing it to retain only a small quantity [of branches] per foot. For ordinary harvests, one can sow melons, like gourds and cucumbers, in the open ground. Left to themselves, they produce a yield that is abundant and usually good. One must observe only that the fruits must be protected from moisture which will make them rot, by putting pieces of tile, slate, or even pieces of plates under them, big enough in every case so that the melon can be supported on it when it is fully grown. This method will protect them from the moisture in the soil and the appetite of insects, which are voracious.

Melons, because of their considerable similarity to cucumbers and pumpkins, are quite liable to degenerate if they are planted too close to the latter plants, because the wind carrying the pollen or fertile dust from these plants to the pistil of the melons will spread their characteristics. While the taste of the melon does not change for this harvest, the resown seed will produce fruit tasting like the cucumbers or pumpkins near the place where the seed was harvested. This is why the seed of a very good melon sometimes produces bad-tasting ones. It is therefore necessary, to always have good melons, after having fertilized your seed with a sure variety, to separate the plants from which you want to preserve the seed from any plant in the same family. It is even good to separate them by one or two rows of corn or other plant tall and leafy enough to prevent all communication of pollen with this square. In this manner you will be certain to preserve your variety pure, except for the changes that the character of the soil may make to the species.

To have the seeds of melons, cucumbers, pumpkins, etc., well developed, one must allow the fruit to rot in place, except for those that survive a long time, which one lets rot in a cellar without attending to them. When the fruits are well rotted, throw the seed into water in a vase, wash it, and store it when it is fully dry. The seed of this family survives a long time.

EGGPLANT

[Fr. *Mélongène;* Lat. *Solanum melongena* L.] This is the same thing as *brehême.* (See *[aubergine].*)

MUSTARD

[Fr. *Moutarde;* Lat. *Sinapsis nigra*] Mustard is sown in the springtime to give seed during the year; one can sow it in any season, if the greens only are wanted, except during frosts, to which it is sensitive.

TURNIPS

[Fr. *Navet;* Lat. *Brassica napus* L.] There are several classifications of turnip, some early, others late. They can be sown from February until October, observing that the earliest ones are not the biggest. The Swiss turnip can serve as food or fodder. Its leaves are eaten like spinach.

Turnips generally like a friable soil; they grow larger in heavy soils, but they are of better quality in light soils.

The turnip of Freneuse and those of Meaux, Belleville, and Vaugirard, sown in the sandy soils on the other side of the lake, would produce a delicious yield.

The large kinds prefer to be planted in the open. The plant does not transplant.

ONIONS

[Fr. *Oignon;* Lat. *Allium cepa* L.] This plant prefers enriched soil, well cultivated and newly manured. In light soil one can sow in January, but in heavy soils one must wait until February or March. It can be sowed again (especially the white onion) in August or September, then thinned in October or November, 3 or 4 inches apart; water in springtime and it will yield sooner and with a better appearance than that sown in March. When sowing in March, sow thinly, in order not to transplant. When the onion has acquired two-thirds of its thickness, the stem must be cut or trimmed; instead of depriving it, this operation will make it grow a lot bigger. You know that the onion is mature when the stem begins to dry out, and when the layers of bulb are well formed and dry. It must be harvested in dry weather, and kept in a cool and dry place if one wants to store it.

SORREL

[Fr. *Oseille;* Lat. *Rumex acetosa*] This is propagated by seed sown in the springtime, or by root divisions separated and transplanted in the spring or fall. Borders of sorrel are put around the flower beds of the garden and around [vegetable] squares. It holds the soil and grows together abundantly. To increase the production of sorrel, cut back its stem before it flowers, and repeat this procedure each time it produces a new stem. The sorrel of Belleville, or those with large leaves, is very good; there is a kind called infertile, which is propagated only by dividing and replanting the root; this is the best. It rarely goes to seed.

PARSNIPS

[Fr. *Panais;* Lat. *Pastinaca sativa* L.] This plant is cultivated like the carrot; it is not averse to frost.

SWEET POTATOES

[Fr. *Patates douces;* Lat. *Convolvulus batatas*] Four kinds of potatoes are grown in Louisiana: the white, which is recognized by its skin and its white flesh; the red, of which the flesh is white under a red skin; the yellow, of which the skin and the flesh are yellow; and the *maroteau* [new potato?] which has red skin and white meat. A fifth kind exists with red skin and white meat, but it has become extremely rare.

Red, yellow and *maroteau* potatoes need a sandy soil. The *maroteau* is the earliest and is ordinarily planted last; one might perhaps pick a good part of this kind for first fruits. Drought does not detract from the quality of the root of these three species; when they languish for lack of water, they do not become more stringy on that account, which must make them preferable when one cannot exert the cares that the white kind exacts. This latter kind is quite the runner by nature, and when its roots do not meet up with obstacles, they elongate without getting larger and become woody and hard.

The appropriate soil for this potato is black earth at the surface, with a base of clay which will arrest the root; the soil does not need to be too new. Whatever kind one grows, one should have well-cultivated soil without clods; prepare it in mounds 18 to 20 inches at the base, with the same height, and a length determined by that of the square [it is in]. The more friable the soil, the more the potatoes will succeed. Choose the smallest and the longest potatoes, and cut into pieces about three inches long. Make holes 5 to 6 inches deep, at the top of the mound, in which put two or three pieces of potato. These holes must be placed two or three feet apart. If you fear drought, make them deeper. Take care to weed carefully until the runner covers the soil entirely, then the weeds will no longer sprout. Potatoes planted in this manner are called *mother potatoes;* those planted in the manner indicated below are called *runners.*

White and red potatoes are planted from the beginning of February into March; they ought not be planted any more by the end of April; it is too late; but the *maroteau* can be planted until the end of May.

The runner potato must be planted in May. For this purpose take runners from the mother potatoes, [and] cut ends two feet long; take three of them for each base, which you fold in two in the middle in such a way that the two ends join, and put them in the ground, planting the fold in a hole made in the mound, so that the two ends stick out. You must choose a rainy spell to perform this transplant, and wait until moisture has well penetrated the mounds. Weed as already noted. The white, yellow, and red runner potatoes are planted until the end of June; the *maroteau* can be planted until the end of August.

The roots of mother potatoes do not store well; those of the runners can be preserved all winter, and even up to the month of May, if stored with care.

To keep these all winter, heap them up under a roof or in the open air so that the pile forms a pyramid; the fatter the pile is, the better they will keep. Cover the pile with a layer of straw, hay, moss, or dry weeds—at least six inches thick—[and] put on top of this cover a layer of earth, thick enough to prevent the entry of air and water, the only enemies to fear.

If the pile is in the open, make a kind of little roof by covering the earth with materials suitable to allow rain water to run off, such as long straw, palmetto leaves, planks, boards, etc., and dig a little ditch around the pile which will carry the water away, and keep the base of the pile as dry as possible.

Sweet potatoes are planted in mounds because the runner roots always seek to extend themselves and become hard and woody when they are free. The effect of the mounds is to arrest the roots, which, forced to enlarge, become more tender, starchy, sugary, and of an exquisite taste.

PARSLEY

[Fr. *Persil;* Lat. *Apium petroselinum* L.] The seed of this plant ordinarily takes forty days to come up. However, it will come up more promptly if one sows it around the time of the summer solstice; this plant is not averse to heat and resists cold well; it is planted in any weather and in any exposure.

BLOODWORT

[Fr. *Pinprenelle;* Lat. *Poterium sanguisorba* L.] This plant is hardly in use, except for garnish in salads. It is sowed in the springtime, but better in autumn. It is propagated again by separating the large clumps and then replanting them; all soils suit it.

LEEKS

[Fr. *Poireau;* Lat. *Allium porrum* L.] Sow in the springtime in well-broken soil; cover the seed with a rake or fork; firm the earth with the foot, or pass the roller; when the plant has acquired enough strength, transplant it into beds in rows 5 to 6 inches apart [and] leave a 4-inch interval between each leek in the row. To perform this operation well, the root of each leek must be cut at about one line from the base, and [at] the ends of the leaves, so that the plant is not more than 6 to 7 inches long. Make, with the planter, some deep holes and let the leeks fall at the same time that you pull out the planter, in such a manner that the earth that falls back covers only the root of the plant, the hole needing to remain open. Watering is necessary; and when the neck of the leek has emerged from the earth, fill up the holes with the hoe. You can mound them up by opening a small furrow with a scribe between each row when the leaves are high enough; this procedure is designed to increase the white part, [an] essential part of the plant. If the leaves of the leek are cut back several times in succession, it will make them enlarge. This plant makes seed only in the second year. It can be sown again in the fall; these will enlarge in the spring, and will succeed others when they go to seed. They are resistant to heavy frost.

PEAS

[Fr. *Pois;* Lat. *Pisum sativum* L.] I have already explained how to deal with this vegetable to get the first fruits. In normal cultivation, the beds are laid out 3 feet wide [and] four furrows are opened in each bed. The peas are sown in the furrows, two together, each pair separated from the other by three to five inches according to the height of the variety. Dwarf peas have little height, and may be scattered in the open, or better in rows or in pockets. Those to be staked must be staked as soon as their tendrils or threads appear. Care is taken to hoe before this procedure, and when they fall down on the footpaths between the beds, they must be pushed back inside the bed, while taking care not to bruise them.

One can begin to sow peas as soon as the fear of frost has passed, and sooner if one can shelter them along a wall or shelving bed. They are sown in several stages to have them throughout the year, but the sowings of June, July, and August succeed with great difficulty because of the great heat. It can even happen that the May planting becomes overheated when, after a strong rain, the sun reappears with force; the plant yellows and the flowers fall off. One can sow again at the end of August and better in September for the early varieties, which can ripen their fruit before winter. One must not plant in earth that has produced peas during the past three years at least, nor in earth newly manured.

POTATOES

[Fr. *Pommes de terre;* Lat. *Solanum tuberosum* L.] Potatoes are planted either by cutting large tubers in as many pieces as there are eyes, or by choosing the smallest ones and planting them whole. Some growers have a punch to remove only the eyes of potato; in this manner they save the tuber. This method succeeds fairly well. One can plant them right after the severe frosts; however, the most appropriate time is March and April. They are planted in rows two feet apart, leaving an interval of fifteen inches between each plant. When the stems have grown a little bit they are mounded up. One can also plant them in mounds, like sweet potatoes. As soon as they begin to drop flowers, cut the stems 4 inches from the ground, to make the tubers swell. To store them, one must not harvest before maturity, which is recognized when the stem dries; but they can be used in all stages of growth. Modern medicine has discovered that the potato, eaten raw, is the most powerful remedy against scurvy. Potatoes are stored, like sweet potatoes, in a heap; one can also put them in well-closed barrels, alternating a layer of very dry sand and a layer of potatoes; the sand layers at the bottom and top of the barrels must be thicker than those in the middle, to protect them from all contact with air and moisture.

PEPPERS

[Fr. *Piment;* Lat. *Capsicum* L.] This plant is sown in beds in January, or in a sheltered flower bed, in February, March, and April. It is transplanted, when it is strong enough, among small vegetables whose growth it will not bother, such as lettuce, endive, etc.

RADISHES, LONG RADISHES

[Fr. *Raves* and *radis;* Lat. *Raphanus sativus oblongus* and *Raphanus sativus rotundus*] These plants are sown in all seasons, but the care must be matched to the time of year. In summer one must sow in the shade; in winter, in hotbeds. These roots being truly good only to the extent that they have rapid growth, one ought always promote their growth either through hotbeds or by irrigation. When the growth of this plant languishes, it becomes hard and stringy and acquires a strong and disagreeable taste.

For the radish to be crisp, its growth must be rapid enough that it gets to the size of a nice filbert when its top has only four to five leaves; in this state its color is fresh, its skin luminous, its root very fine and without hair. In hardening, the root enlarges, makes hairs, the color turns, and its fine, light spicy taste changes into a bitter taste which catches sometimes in the throat.

White radishes are the earliest, and the red are the most agreeable to look at, but all kinds are good. Long radishes are ordinarily more watery than common radishes.

WILD ROCKET

[Fr. *Roquette;* Lat. *Brassica eruca* L.] Sown in the spring and fall, this plant is not difficult as to terrain nor exposure. It must be sown thinly or be transplanted.

SALSIFY

[Fr. *Salsifis;* Lat. *Tragopogon porrifollium* L.] This root is planted from the beginning of spring until the end of autumn, in friable, but not newly manured soil. It must be watered frequently until the seed has come up. It does not go to seed until the second year.

SCORZONERA (BLACK SALSIFY OR VIPER'S GRASS)

[Fr. *Scorsonère;* Lat. *Scorsonera hispanica*] This is cultivated the same, but it has an advantage over salsify; it is a triennial and its roots remain tender, even when the plant is making seed.

To have beautiful scorzonera, do not touch it the first year. The second, the roots will be very large, and if one removes the stems just when they flower, they will be preserved until the third year.

ESCAROLE

[Fr. *Scarole;* Lat. *Cickorium endiva latifolia*] Escarole is grown like chicory and resists the heat of summer well.

TOMATO

[Fr. *Tomate, pomme d'amour;* Lat. *Lycopersicon*] Plant in hotbeds beginning in January or February; transplant into the open ground, in a full exposure; support the stems, which are flexible, with stakes, and water in dry weather. Many species are known, all of which are used in cooking and are equally good.

One can cover a wall or partition with these, or the base of an arbor, where they will create a rather lovely effect from the tender green of the leaves and the red emanating from the fruit.

JERUSALEM ARTICHOKE, OR EARTH PEAR

[Fr. *Topinambour;* Lat. *Helianthus tuberosus* L.] This is propagated either by putting the little tubers back into the ground in the month of October, or by seeds sown in the springtime. This plant ordinarily renews itself through the fragments of root remaining in the ground after it is harvested. Some people seek it for the taste of the tubers, which is very close to that of artichoke hearts.

One can use it as an ornamental; its flowers resemble those of the sunflower, but are smaller.

INSTRUCTIONS ON
SOWING SEEDS

➤─┤◆➤─◇─◆┤─◄

The largest portion of seeded plants are sown to be transplanted later; therefore, you must put your young plant into a condition to undergo this operation; that is to say, its root must have hairs. For this purpose, do not sow in the open ground, because most of your plants will make only a taproot without capillary roots, and they will droop a great deal when you transplant them. Since all seeds do not need the warmth of a hotbed to sprout, it is useless to plant all of them there, but sow them in well-decomposed humus reduced to light soil. Your seed, finding itself comfortable there, will develop a large quantity of hair roots, which will give it the strength to take root easily in the place where you transplant it.

When your compost is ready, either in a box, or on the very ground, provided that it is six inches thick, throw the seed over it. Then dust some more very fine humus over it, more or less according to the size of the seed, from the thickness of a 25-*sous* coin for small seeds up to a finger for the largest. Keep your soil reasonably and continuously moist, [and] increase the watering when the plant begins to get stronger, at least for plants not averse to water, like wallflower, annual wallflower, etc.

When the plant has achieved a certain size, and has sprouted several leaves, pull it up with a trowel or transplanter, and separate each base while gently managing the root hairs; then replant each division at reasonable intervals, according to the size that the plant will attain, and water this new plant well: it is also necessary to protect it from sun for nine days, and each evening give it a light sprinkling, if you notice the plants have been drooping. Too much water weakens and rots them, too much dryness stunts and kills them. It would be appropriate then to do the transplanting during rainy weather, but there are dry seasons that do not permit this; then one must have recourse to irrigation. The plant, so grown and enlarged, is lifted in a clump of earth to be transplanted into flower beds or into a parterre. When one performs this last operation, one must create a kind of basin around the newly placed plant, by forming a ring with the earth, and flood it, so to speak, as soon as one has finished replanting it. Take great care with it for ten to fifteen days. One assumes that the soil where the plant is transplanted into its place will be well cultivated and free of weeds, which one must take care to destroy as soon as they appear.

A plant difficult to root in the ground must be raised in a small pot, its roots enlarging and shaping around the inside of the pot. To transplant, depot it and put the entire clump into the ground, without cutting off anything; it will tolerate this operation without drooping too much. To depot a plant, withhold water for at least two days, so that the dried soil will contract into a solid clump. Soil too wet will fall away from the root; soil too dry will crumble into powder.

COMMENTS ON SEEDS

Frequently we are too hasty in accusing the seed that fails to come up as being of bad quality. It happens that after waiting more than a year for the germination of certain seeds, and having emptied the pots that contained them into the garden, one sees them germinate in a short space of time and develop rapidly. That is because the seeds did not encounter, when they were sown, the combination of circumstances necessary for their development. Too much or too little care, water, or heat; a bad or inappropriate exposure for the plant; and poorly timed planting of the seed are causes of suspending germination. When a seed has not sprouted in the amount of time expected, it must be resown, with all the attention possible, and the most favorable exposure sought with care for the plant one is sowing. It is good to observe that in the course of this work, when I mention a full exposure, I mean towards the south, as the most favorable for growth.

I have indicated in the Gardener's Almanac the time to sow different seeds; it remains for me to observe that, when one sows in too dry weather, the seed does not come up. In this case one must soak the seed in sulfured water until the germ appears; one will sow that in soil well watered for the preceding two or three days, maintain a heavy moisture level until the complete development of the plant, [and] then moderate the watering, in order not to weaken it.

One must avoid, in every case, watering during the heat of the day, under pain of seeing the plants scorch. The most appropriate time is after sunset or early in the morning.

DETAILS FROM PARIS NURSERYMAN VILMORIN'S
ADVERTISEMENTS FOR CABBAGES.
(Translator's collection)

Early York cabbage

Sugarloaf cabbage

Quintal cabbage

PROPAGATION OF
VEGETABLES

⊱⊱⊶⊶⊙⊷⊷⊰⊰

The [two] methods of propagating vegetables are natural or artificial. Natural methods are [by] *Seeds, Offsets, Offshoots,* and *Pods.*

Everyone knows what are called seeds; offsets, in bulbous plants, are small bulbs that sprout from the neck of the root around the principal bulb. Offshoots, or eyelets, are little plants similar in every respect to the mother plant, produced by the root, which grow around the main stem and can be separated without harming the mother plant. We ordinarily apply the name *eyelet* to the sprouts of herbaceous plants, that of *offshoots* to woody plants.

Pods are produced by some plants only; these are a kind of offset bulb which, instead of growing from the neck of the root of bulbous plants, grows at the ends of the stems, in place of seed. All of these natural products, separated from the mother plant and placed in the ground, produce a completely similar plant; it is the best method of preserving the species pure, seeds nearly always making them vary.

Artificial means are *Cuttings, Layers,* and *Grafts.*

Cuttings are branches or roots detached from a plant and transplanted in conditions appropriate to make them take root. These conditions are a friable and substantial soil, kept continuously moist, often also in modest warmth, without being exposed too much to the rays of the sun.

To make cuttings one must break the branch [bending the upper part] like a heel, or cutting below a node or button, horizontally, clean, with a well-sharpened and appropriate tool. (If making cuttings from different plants at the same time, it is necessary to wash the blade carefully before passing from one plant to the other, because the juice of one plant is often a poison to another.)

Pull the leaves off the cutting up to two-thirds of its length, beginning at the bottom, taking care not to wound the bark; pinch off the end if the branch was destined to flower soon.

Cuttings are planted with attention: (1) to leave two or three eyes, or the crown of leaves above ground; (2) to separate the cuttings enough so that one can move them easily in clumps, after they have rooted; (3) not to insert them into the earth with too much force, because possibly encountering a hard surface, the bark will be wounded, or even torn off, which will cause the cutting to fail. Make a hole with the thumb or with a stick bigger than the branch, place the cutting very straight, and mound earth up against it by pressing lightly with the two first fingers of each hand; then water abundantly at first, and thereafter maintain moderate but constant moisture.

With plants that are difficult to root and that need heat, one puts them in hotbeds, under glass, or under a cold frame. Sometimes also one settles for inverting a drinking glass, a widemouthed jar, a bottle shard, etc., over it, which is removed when it is certain that the plant has taken root.

Not all cuttings want to be put in the ground as soon as they are separated from the mother plant, such as cuttings of thick-leaved plants or succulents, like prickly pear, pineapple, etc. So one must let them dry, until the sap no longer seeps out of the cut or end, because the oozing of sap into the earth would rot the plant.

With very thick-leaved plants, one must put them in sand until they have made their first roots, then move them in clumps into more substantial soil.

When a plant is averse to being propagated in this manner, make a ligature on the branch chosen for the cutting with a waxed thread or a brass wire. The object of this technique is to block the sap, which, by its downward flow, forms an excrescence above the tourniquet. When the clot is well formed, as has been explained, cut above it; the roots will grow from this point, if the cuttings are planted with the precautions prescribed above.

Cuttings of some moisture-loving plants such as oleander, grape-vines, etc. prefer to be prepared in water. Some people are in the habit of twisting the base of the cutting, or slitting it to introduce a barley or oat seed. These methods are harmful in that the wounds that are made on the plant do nothing but alter it by disposing the bark to rot from the bruising that it undergoes from being twisted, and the seed cannot provide any nourishment to the plant in which it is imprisoned by the roots that it sprouts, since, most often, it is completely incongruous; on the contrary, it absorbs the juices which the cutting needs for nourish-ment; also we always observe the soil becoming thin, and the cutting languishes.

Layers serve to propagate trees and shrubs, and are made by choos-ing, from a stock, a branch that can be laid down on the earth. The leaves are removed from the point where it will be inserted into the ground, a cut is made below and across in mid-wood, [and] this incision is continued about one inch in the upper part, following the direction of the pith. An oblique trench is dug in previously cultivated earth, the branch is laid down in it, and [it] is secured by means of a little hook inserted into the ground below the spot of the incision. The upper part of the branch is straightened in a perpendicular direction, so that the cut portion detaches from the mother plant, and forms a right angle with it; it is [then] re-covered with earth and watered. From the cut end, the roots will take life. It is easy to understand that layers succeed better than cuttings, because the branch embedded in such a manner is not deprived of the sap of the plant to which it adheres, a part only being detached, and it is because that part is deprived of the sap of the mother plant that it makes roots.

Rambling plants, such as vines, can do without the incision. It suffices to lay a branch in the ground; the following year one can cut it; it will be provided with a large quantity of hair roots.

Not all plants lend themselves to layering, either because of their fragility, or because of the height of the stem. [For these] make a ligature, as for cuttings, at the branch that you want to layer, insert this branch in a pot pierced in the bottom, so as to put the ligature a third or halfway up the height of the pot, which is filled with potting soil; support the pot with pickets, secure it well, and keep the soil constantly moist. Cut the branch below the pot when the plant has taken root; this new plant may remain in the pot or be removed in a clump for transplanting elsewhere. People who make a lot of these kinds of layers have pots sawed in two, or [they use] two-piece boxes designed so that they can be set close to the branches; the two parts are held together with a cord.

Observe that in every case involving a ligature or incision, it must be made immediately below a node or eye, no other part of the plant being able to put out roots.

To graft a tree is to transfer onto [it] a part of another more preferable species, which is implanted on it [and] grows at its expense, without changing its nature, and without the [original] tree being changed. This technique, practiced from time immemorial, has for its purpose to perpetuate some fruit species, which are lost in sowing their seeds, [and] to obtain more beautiful, larger, juicier, and tastier fruits.

Grafting is practiced in many ways, but the most common are cleft, shield bud, and approach grafts.

The cleft graft is made at the moment when the sap begins to rise (February and March). Cut some small branches from the latest growth of the tree of which you want to propagate the variety, keeping a little bit of wood from the preceding growth. These branches can be saved several days in a cool place without moisture, which secures the advantage of transporting them afar.

On the stock that you want to graft, choose a spot where the bark is quite smooth and without nodes. Cut the head of the stock cleanly and horizontally; then, using a hacksaw or strong knife and a mallet, cut the stock near the pith; trim the graft into a bevel at the intersection of the young wood and the old, at the level of an eye, taking care to flatten the cut on one side so as to remove all of the bark from this side and to leave it on the other; hold the crevice of the stock open with the help of a wooden coin; adjust the graft which has been refreshed on the upper end by being matched on the exterior edge of its bark exactly to the bark of the stock, pull out the coin, and the crevice will close around the graft. To protect it from intemperate weather, wrap the head of the stock and the foot of the graft (which must have two or three eyes outside, above the stock), with a well-stirred mixture of two parts resin and one wax, and apply it with a flat stick or tamp. For big trees cover the cut with thick clay applied with a rag, so that neither rain nor drought will make it fall.

For shield bud grafting, branches with good eyes formed in the spring are cut from the [preceding] year's growth, when the trees are in full sap (June or July), from the species chosen for propagation; the leaves are removed near where they connect to the stem, one eye sufficing for each graft.

The bud is raised by incising the branch in a double bevel as far as the middle of the woody part, beginning from several lines above the eye to several lines below;* the eye is detached from the branch by passing a piece of horsehair folded in two between the wood and the bark

---

*A grafter, a small knife with polished and perfectly sharp blade is used, with a handle of horn or ivory terminating with a small bone or ivory plate in the form of a spatula.

with the two ends run through your buttonhole. Holding the woody branch in one hand, the bark in the other, pushing lightly, the eye will lift off perfectly. If it should happen that the eye remains empty, the bud is worthless and cannot be used. When you are assured that the eye is good, cut the bark squarely a line or two above the eye, without touching the lower part, which will give it somewhat the shape of a shield.

With the bud so prepared, put it in your mouth, holding it by the leaf stem, then make a double incision on the stock in the form of a T; spread open the bark on the two upper sides of the incision with the grafting spatula; then introduce the bud with the point down so that it adheres well and the bark recovers it entirely. This done, tie the whole thing together with a string, or better with a wool thread, tightening slightly so as not to cut off the flow of the sap, but enough to prevent the bark from opening. [Since] this graft must be executed very quickly, one would do well to practice ahead of time on stocks of little importance, in order to acquire the dexterity necessary for success.

Oranges are grafted the same, but with the precaution of shaping the bud so that the point is on the upper side, and the incision on the stock is made in a reverse T, because moisture being genuinely poisonous to this tree, water will be introduced less easily into the notch. But whatever the form and disposition of the bud, it always needs to be set with the eye toward the sky; so for oranges, it will have the point at the top and above the eye, and will be cut squarely below; this will be the inverse [of the procedure] for other trees. Delicate shrubs are side-grafted ["by approach"]. This graft is impracticable for trees situated far away from each other; but if the variety that one wants to propagate is in a box or pot, it will be easy to put it next to the stock one wants to graft.

One must choose a branch with a thickness exactly equal to that of the stock, [and] notch both the stock and the graft obliquely, as far as the middle of the pith (without depriving either one of its top), align the two cut pieces exactly, and tie them together with thread, twine, etc. When you are sure that the two parts are quite welded, cut the branch of the tree that you want to propagate in several places below the [level of the] joint. After so severing the graft, cut back the original top of the stock, so that all the sap goes to the graft.

When the grafts have sprouted well and you are sure they have rooted, take care to cut off all the suckers that should grow on the tree below the graft, because in addition to these suckers not matching the species of the [new] graft, they use up the sap which it needs to develop.

One cannot graft one tree to another indifferently. They must be similar enough to be classed in the same genus or at least in the same family.

With fruit trees, one must always graft kernel fruit to kernel fruit and stone fruit to stone fruit. One grafts all kinds of roses onto eglantine or wild rose, as well as onto the white thorn;[7] the medlar[8] is ordinarily grafted on this last stock.

It is well to decide, in grafting, whether one wants to have dwarf or tall-trunked trees, in order to choose appropriate stocks. For dwarf trees, graft upon quince, *paradis,* and on frail stocks, ordinarily not growing tall; while for tall trunks one must choose fine stocks, vigorous species that ordinarily grow tall; choose good wood eyes for the bud, and then prune them according to their destination.

Shield bud grafting on dormant eyes is done in the month of September; this is called the dormant eye graft, because it does not sprout during the winter, but in the springtime, when the sap rises.

Nurserymen ordinarily sell grafted trees; but since it can become advantageous to substitute for the species that the tree rests on another more attractive, more productive, or better acclimated species, I must warn that one can graft a tree several times, graft on graft. This method is indeed employed by many growers, with the aim of obtaining more abundant and beautiful fruit; the effect of the graft being to constrict the circulation of the sap, it flows to greater advantage, which augments production, but always at the expense of the stock; also it is noteworthy, that a tree grafted several times does not live as long as one grafted only once, and that one not as long as one not grafted [at all]. If one grafts a very young stock, it will come into fruit earlier than one grafted at an older age, but also it will not live as long.

✧ OBSERVATIONS ✦

Trees in the open are grafted when they have acquired a circumference of four to five inches; the graft is placed five or six feet up, [and] the sprouts are cut back to form a crown later.

Half-standard trunks, not as tall as those in the open, are grafted lower; bulrushes, bushes, and espaliers are grafted three to five inches from the ground.

When one buds a seed-bearing plant (a plant produced from a seed), it can be done at ground level; but if the tree is intended for the open, one must preserve the principal shoot of the graft, and grow it until it attains the height one considers appropriate; then one makes it head by cutting it back to the height wanted.

FRUIT TREES

⊱─┼─◈─┼─◈─○─◈─┼─◈─┼─⊰

Fruit trees, very much neglected in Lower Louisiana because of the lack of success of some growers, nevertheless merit our attention. It is astounding that a country so rich in vegetation should be deprived of the succulent fruits that provide delicacies not only in the North, but in countries much farther south than New Orleans. The Antilles, for example, have nearly all the fruits of Europe, along with those of hot countries; does not Louisiana seem more appropriate to northern fruits, since even oranges are hard put to produce here? Some well-directed attempts will suffice to prove the possibility of establishing productive orchards, which will furnish fresh fruits as good as and perhaps better than those brought from Baton Rouge, Pointe Coupée, etc. The nearness of these places is a guarantee of the success than can be obtained in this kind of cultivation.

Apple trees grow wild in the woods, where they are covered with a small, bitter fruit good only for preserves; it was the same with the best rennet [pippin apple] before they were brought under cultivation. This science modifies, improves, and refines the species; there is no wild fruit it cannot make edible. Here, there is no need for complex science to achieve this end, since grafting offers the means of implanting a delicious variety in turn onto a tree that is native to the country. Some enthusiasts have in their gardens apple trees which bear very beautiful and very good fruit, of which the species can become acclimated; from this one can conclude that it is possible to achieve a widespread and happy result, when one wants to take the trouble. What I have said of the

119

apple can be applied to the pear, which grafts well on the apple; [and] of the cherry, of which every variety can be grafted on the wild cherry tree of the country. I regard as sufficiently proved that the peach can succeed, according to the results obtained by several growers who possess excellent varieties of it. Finally, the necessity of having tasty and healthful fruit is so well appreciated that I am persuaded that many people would devote themselves to this culture, if they were familiar with its principles. That is why I am going to give instruction on the planting and pruning of trees; if they might be useful to some people desirous of giving to their country some agreeable produce of which nature is prodigious elsewhere, I will have achieved my purpose; my efforts will be sufficiently rewarded.

CULTIVATION OF FRUIT TREES

Trees imported from northern states or from Europe are ordinarily grafted. For them to develop, it suffices to plant them in favorable circumstances, give them some care during their growing period, and nature will do the rest.

PLANTING

If the trees have suffered during transport, they will have lost their freshness; the bark of the upper sprouts will be shriveled, sometimes dry, and the tree's principal arms or branches will be affected more or less according to how much the tree has suffered.

The first responsibility is to inspect the roots [and] remove those that are torn or badly bruised. Trim the good ones back to live tissue, [and] suppress all those that are dry, by cutting them with a very sharp tool, just to the base of the tree; then put the base in water for two or three days. Root pruning must always be done on the underside, because if it were done above, water from rain or irrigation would filter in between the wood and the bark, rotting them.

While the trees are soaking one can prepare the place chosen for them. Make holes three to five feet square, and at least three feet deep; if the earth is moist, put in a foot of plaster or other material that is good for promoting drainage; then replace the soil, up to about a foot from the level of the earth. When removing the trees from the water to plant them, one must carefully inspect the branches, cut back all those that are dry, and cut back the others as close to the trunk as you can without distorting the top.

Refill the cavity in such a manner that in placing the tree on the earth, the level up to where it had previously been planted is not more than a half inch below the surface of the ground, while turning the graft to the south side. Hold the tree very straight, perpendicularly, while throwing well-crumbled soil over the roots. When they have been covered, gently shake the tree by moving it up and down, so that the roots are sure to take their natural position. If there are some that are too flexible, which bend under the weight of the soil, arrange them with the hand, in a horizontal direction. Press the soil lightly with the foot, and fill the hole completely. Whatever kind of tree one plants, one must always avoid burying the graft. If it is dry, dig a basin around the base of the tree, and water copiously; it is good, in any case, to water after planting; the earth, being washed by the water into little cavities, presses better against the roots, making the rooting of the tree more certain.

When trees are very fresh one can dispense with the soaking, and be content with trimming the roots and branches. Trees [destined for] the open are not pruned, except to remove dead or superfluous wood.

In cold and temperate countries, the best fruits are trained in espalier. (That is what we call trees planted along a wall, to which the branches are attached); this method of planting and managing trees produces the advantage of [being able to] choose the wood one wants to retain and cutting off all that is either unnecessary or of bad quality; also, the fruits of espaliers are much superior to fruits [of trees] in the open, both in volume and in flavor.

In this area where properties are not enclosed with walls, espaliers cannot be used, but one can plant trees on trellises, which will produce the same advantage.

Trellises are constructed by inserting strong posts in the ground, of an indefinite height and at a distance convenient for receiving two cross pieces above and below, on which one attaches little poles either horizontally, or better perpendicularly, or lastly in lattice shapes. These poles or lathes are nailed or attached with a tie of tempered brass wire. Trees that one plants against these trellises must be inclined, the graft above; that is to say, instead of planting them perpendicularly and touching the trellis, one distances the root by bending the tree, in such a manner that it forms a 30- to 45-degree angle on the horizontal. The purpose of this inclination is to frustrate the sap, which in a tree planted straight tends always to put out strong wood shoots and few fruit branches. One must prune the tree as soon as it is planted, so that the flow of the sap turns entirely to the profit of the branches that are to be retained. The distance to mark between each tree base must be relative to the fertility of the soil and to the species, compared to the size that the tree ordinarily attains; this distance varies from twelve to twenty feet, and more. Those that extend the most are the peach grafted onto the almond, the apricot, the plum Queen Claude [greengage], and several varieties of pears. As for the exposure [required], it is almost indifferent if one plants in *treillage,* since air and heat circulate freely on all sides; however, it would be good to plant toward the south or east, because of the tendency that vegetation has to sprout preferentially on the side where it receives sun. But if one wants to plant against the exterior walls of a house, it is appropriate then to suit the species to the exposure. Grapevines, Good Christian winter pears, royal winter pears, late peaches such as Venus breast, the *bourdine,* the belle of Vitry, purple peaches, and nectarines like a southern exposure.

East is appropriate for grapevines, peaches, apricots, and early pears; it is the best exposure.

West is appropriate for all pears [and] for grapevines, which will ripen their fruits in that exposure less quickly than in the two preceding ones.

Finally north is suitable for fruit of which one wants to delay the maturity, in order to enjoy the produce of one's garden for a longer time; but it must be noted that the fruit does not have as much flavor as it does in the three other exposures. I would counsel people who are interested in fruit that is rare in this country to plant cherry trees here, and gooseberries; this will be a means of acclimating them.

When one would plant grapevines on a trellis, one would do well to grow the base of a single stem up to the height of the posts, then divide it into two arms, which one runs along a strand on each side; the growth produced by numerous ramblers that it puts out each year, in addition to making a pretty effect, will be advantageous to the fruit trees below them by providing them some shade against the scorching rays of the summer sun.

WOOD AND FRUIT BRANCHES AND BUDS

Before passing on to the principles of pruning, it is good to make known the different kinds of branches and buds that might be met on a tree. The buds or eyes are of two sorts, woody and fruity. The woody kind are elongated; fruit buds are fat and round. By visual inspection one can judge, after the leaves fall, if a tree is going to produce a lot of fruit, since the eyes that will produce it are very apparent and easy to recognize by their form. One can also judge which are the wood buds, which ought to produce the most vigorous shoots; these are big and full while maintaining their elongated form; while those that are destined to give birth to fruit shoots and twigs are small and thin.

Gardeners classify a somewhat large number branch varieties, of which more than a half are divisions of the principal branches, which is why I count only four kinds: wood branches, fruit branches, twigs, and suckers.

Wood branches are those that have fine well-nourished wood eyes not too close together. These branches are of medium thickness and sprout naturally on the last eye of the last pruning cut.

Fruit branches are ordinarily not as big as the preceding, not as long, and adorned with fruit eyes at the base. Twigs are small, thin, elongated branches; they should be retained only to the extent that they are well placed and better ones are lacking. Suckers sprout somewhat normally through the bark of the tree's principal branches; they are large at the bottom and well nurtured even when emerging; their base uses nearly all of the capacity of the branch from which they emerge; they sprout, elongating and growing as if all at once; usually they get to be several feet long in a summer. Their skin is normally brown, above all at the base; their eyes are small, rare; their bark is rough.

PRUNING OF TREES

The purpose of pruning is to give the tree an elegant form, to make it produce the most copious and beautiful fruit possible without exhausting it, to hasten its growth, and to prolong its existence.

Since the same method of pruning is not appropriate for all trees indifferently, and the principles should vary according to their nature and [growing] habits, I am going to present, for each kind, the methods used by the masters in this art.

Since sap flows naturally in a perpendicular direction, all trees tend to grow upwards and make a lot of wood. Experience has proved that in imparting to the branches a direction approaching the horizontal, accompanied by a light bending, the sap, opposed in its flow, produces fewer wood branches and more fruit branches. An espaliered or trellised tree does not need to be full of woody branches; therefore in its youth only four principal branches, which are called arms, need to be preserved. These are directed laterally by being attached to the poles or lattices that form the trellis; the two lowest nearly horizontally, the two in the middle higher, but bent lightly, to dispose them to take the appropriate direction. This bending must always be applied to the young branches intended to fill out the tree, while not allowing the branches to descend below their point of emergence, because the sap being too much opposed would ooze through the bark and give rise to suckers, which one ought to prevent from growing.

This principle applies to every kind of tree, but is amenable to modifications according to the natural habits of some. When one notices a tree always tending to reassume the perpendicular direction by putting out vigorous woody branches from the upper eyes of the mother branches, one must cut it back a little, in such a way as not to harm its development.

Among all fruit trees the peach demands the most attention to pruning. To form it well, one must guide it from its earliest youth and monitor it in all the seasons of its growth.

The first year of its planting, having chosen a good shoot, cut it back to four or six eyes from the graft. Each eye will produce a branch. Choose the four best or most well-placed ones, the two uppermost being attached in the form of a slightly opened V to form the principal branches; the two lower ones being bent down a little more, in order to fill out the base of the tree. If the tree has sprouted six equally strong and vigorous branches, one should retain them, arranging them in a triple V, in order to take advantage of the bounty of nature. Direct the young shoots in the month of May by staking them. Staking is to tie the branches in the direction they need to occupy, without pruning them.

One must not bend down the mother branches of a pear tree too low, because, since this tree tends toward the vertical more than any other, too much bending will harm its growth; so to fill out the base of the tree, lower the branches each year to the extent that it develops.

The second year one will observe the branches coming out of the eyes left at the time of the first pruning; if the shoot is vigorous, one will prune the branches slightly longer, but never beyond the strong to the weak, that is to say, as far as the place where the branch obviously begins to diminish in thickness, which is ordinarily at the half point or at two-thirds of its length. If the shoot is weak, it must be pruned short, from a fifth to a fourth or a third of its length and as much as possible on a good eye on the lower side. By pruning short, one forces the sap to redescend in the branch, which takes strength, and gets [it] into condition to make more vigorous shoots; but if one pruned short a very vigorous shoot one would run the risk of making it sprout suckers. One must always cut immediately above a good, free wood eye; this is how to make it produce beautiful sprouts, and to form the tree quickly.

Attach the branches to the poles forming the trellises with young willow shoots, rush, strips of palmetto leaves, or even with twigs. Tighten the fibers enough so that the branch does not move around, but not too much, to avoid constricting the branch and having it form a ring.

It happens frequently enough that the tree does not sprout regularly, that is to say, that only one or two vigorous shoots emerge; in this case, one must bend them down severely, while keeping the weakest ones straight (unless these are twigs, because in that case they must be suppressed), [and] prune them to two or three eyes only; [then] balance can be reestablished; but if the weak branches do not strengthen upon the second pruning, they must be eliminated, and the strong ones straightened while cutting them back; they will then produce the wood needed to form the tree.

Every espaliered or trellised tree should be so treated during the two first years.

Dwarf trees, bulrush types, and shrub types must be cut back to six eyes at the most, at the time of planting, and the number of branches necessary for the formation of the tree retained the second year according to the form one wants to give it.

If it happened that, in heavy soil, the tree sprouted only a sucker, it would be difficult to correct this fault; nevertheless, one ought to retain it, trim it very long, and bend the end of the branch to prevent the sap from rising [in it] a second time.

When the tree has acquired the principal arms or branches for its formation, one should think about fruit; each year retain the shoots needed to fill the spaces between the arms, [and] prune for fruit those destined to make fruit-bearing shoots. It is recognized that in seed-bearing trees, the two or three terminal buds form woody branches, the lower eyes making support shoots and buds for fruit; according to this observation, one can modify the pruning according to need.

Do not prune branches that are only two or three inches long, because these branches ordinarily having only one wood bud at the end, and all the lower ones being for fruit, one could not take advantage of this if the sole bud that is indispensable to them for fruiting is cut back; because in order to be productive a fruit bud must be accompanied by a wood bud, or at least by a leaf bud.

Weak or thin branches are pruned to a fourth of their length, that is to say that one cuts back three-fourths.

Those of a medium diameter are pruned in half, if they are 18 to 24 inches long, or to a fourth if their length exceeds this measure.

I have already noted that it is necessary to trim suckers long. Those that without being suckers have disproportionate strength must be pruned the same, so that the circulation of the sap, being slowed on this side, becomes more active near the weak parts of the tree which, for that purpose, will be pruned short.

When the tree has attained its full development, and when the space it should occupy is well filled in, one must, when pruning, cut on a weak branch; the new shoot will be formed using less vigor.

Sometimes the strong branches fill their new shoots and their lower parts with numerous fruit buds; one must then prune long as far as the second or third wood eye; if not, the sprouting of the branch would be arrested.

This kind of pruning, particularly applicable to the peach, suits the apricot equally. However, as the latter is subject to losing its leaves quickly, it is well to prune it shorter and to encourage replacement branches for it.

Everything that has just been said relates only to winter pruning, but trees can be pruned in another method, called summer pruning, or more commonly, *palissage*.[9] This second pruning is effected in May or June, and particularly aids in directing the sap toward the part one wants to strengthen; well-managed disbudding accelerates the formation of the tree; this must be continued until October. *Palissage* consists in suppressing buds that are badly placed, crossed, or too feeble; [and] in arresting those that sprout too vigorously, by pinching the terminal shoots in the case of trees with stone fruits; and in cutting, breaking off, or twisting the twigs and fruit shoots in kernel fruit trees, to make fruit buds grow.

PALISSAGE

When several buds sprout one next to the other, one must detach the weakest ones, preferably those in the rear, if they are almost equal. This suppressing must be done when they are two or three inches long; they are detached easily by pushing from above, being then very tender. One must carefully examine those that develop on the front of the tree; these are ordinarily fruit branches; in that case retain them; but if one notices that they want to grow large, they will have to be suppressed, because wood branches sprouting there would give the tree an ungraceful shape. Since those that grow on the sides produce wood or fruit branches, they are all kept, but with the precaution of pruning the weakest ones to two or three eyes to make them develop fruit buds.

When trees are quite vigorous, only double buds need be suppressed, at the base of the shoot, those sprouting in the front, in the rear, and in the axils of the branches. All of those that are well placed are retained, no matter how numerous, until the month of August (this is a method of allaying the sap), then all the branches are spaced, being directed into the voids to embellish the tree.

When the branches have acquired enough form to be attached, they are fixed in the space they are to occupy, but without being cut back.

The upper side of the branches being more favorable for growth than the lower side, the buds of this side will take on more growth than those on the other, if one does not impede them; to promote an equal distribution of the sap, disbud the upper side a fortnight before the lower side, pinching the buds that want to get carried away, in order to delay them; the lower buds will profit from the delay that this operation forces on the others and will become stronger.

The wood buds of a peach tree develop into branches the second year at the latest, or die out. Because of this, one must consider replacements to avoid having the tree loose its fullness.

Its wood being soft and malleable, exert particular attention in pruning so that the cut does not dry out, and so that it recovers as soon as possible. Begin cutting on the side opposite the eye that will become the terminal shoot, and at about half of its height, and come to the end at about a line above the point of the eye; in this manner the cut will recover without any part drying out.

Peach trees demand assiduous care during their entire growing season; one has to attend them at least once a week, to cut back all the buds that may appear bad, to pinch the young sprouts that may want to grow too quickly, etc.

If a mother branch makes buds only on the upper side, without developing on the underside, it is because the branch is too low; in that case one must detach it [from the paling] and straighten it up; by pinching the buds to retard them, one will force eyes to come out on the opposite side.

In spite of the care that one may have given the tree, it could happen that a branch gets carried away and behaves like a sucker. In that case, when pruning cut it at a lower eye and choose the puniest to establish the pruning; this terminal eye will make only one feeble sprout and balance will be reestablished.

✧ PRUNING PLUM AND CHERRY TREES ✧

These trees are ordinarily planted in the open, but one can train them into espaliers, in a northern exposure, above all the cherry, to protect it from the scorching rays of the sun, which are difficult for it; this will be a means of acclimating this delicious fruit. I have already recommended grafting the cherry on the wild cherry of the countryside, but to procure the grafting stocks it is indispensable to raise some stocks grafted from good species.

Plant toward the northeast, against a wall, the tree of which species you have chosen to propagate by grafting; manage it according to the principles already indicated; arrange the first shoots in a fan shape; these trees will take root easily. Their fruit branches are always very short and last a long time. As these branches do not occupy very much space, increase the number of arms or principal branches as much as you can. In the end this pruning consists principally in the suppression of branches that cannot be attached to the stakes, either because there is no room for them or because they are badly placed, and in the shortening or suppression of those that will starve the others or which destroy the balance. In general one does not need to shorten the staked branches except to force them to develop their lateral eyes into fruit branches. All those that sprout ahead of time are suppressed, if there is no need for them, or are pruned to the thickness of a piece of four *escalins* to obtain several fruit branches.

➤ PRUNING PEAR AND APPLE TREES ❦

Pear and apple trees are pruned in a palmetto shape, which is the arrangement that seems most favorable for them. The tree must be grafted close to the ground, and the graft must have only one year of growth.

Cut [the tree] back the first year, in such a way that at least three well-placed eyes remain; the buds that sprout from the two lower eyes will form the two first arms, and the upper bud will be trained vertically to elongate the stem. If it should develop a larger number, only the three most vigorous would be retained. Attach the uppermost shoot; the two side ones will remain free until autumn, so that they acquire as much strength as possible; then attach them horizontally while they still have some flexibility. In the spring of the second year, detach your tree to cut back the twigs that may remain above the sprouting point of the vertical shoot. Always manage the pruning so that the horizontal branches are separated from one another by 6 to 7 inches, and alternated as equally as possible. So, if the bud on the side where you are waiting for a sprout should not develop, arc the branch vertically in such a way that the eye you want to develop is at the highest point of the arc; in this position it will put out a strong bud; but as soon as symmetry is reestablished, you must straighten out the stem again.

Should the eyes of the lateral branches develop into wood branches, one would convert them into sprigs by pinching them on the stakes. In short, one must procure two lateral branches each year, and prolong the vertical at the same time that one promotes the elongation of the arms already obtained, until the tree has attained the desired development; practice disbudding at vigorous eyes to suppress those that grow too much at the beginning, or that create confusion, observing that the branches be six inches apart—they do not need to cross over each other; because of that, one must prune them long, so that they sprout only fruit branches and twigs.

However, if a branch should die, one should cross the nearest neighbor over to fill the void.

✦ PRUNING IN PYRAMIDS ✦

This is formed on a short trunk (tree grafted low) by cutting it back to 5 or 6 inches, and retaining 3 or 4 buds on it to form the lateral branches and the stem. It is essential to obtain these first buds, because it is from them only that the pyramid will draw its beauty in filling out the bottom, a thing it is impossible to remedy after the stem has already made a certain amount of growth. Oppose the development of any other branch. Arrest the growth of the middle stem each year at 15 or 18 inches, when it gets to this height, in order to give more strength to the lateral branches, trained horizontally in stages each year. In pruning, one cuts them back more or less according to the vigor of the tree and considering the need for a proportionate distribution of the sap among all the branches. Prune at a bud located on top of the branch when you want to change its direction, or at a bud located below if you want to lower the branch, and on the right or left side to move it away even a little bit from the opposite side.

The lower branches always being a year older than the ones above them, since each year a level of branches must form, it results that the tree is shaped into a pyramid. The more it approaches this form the more attractive it is, and it is a sign that the pruning has been well managed.

Pyramids produce much fruit and last a long time. Only pears and apples are subjected to this method; the plum and the cherry may be trained into a palmetto shape.

I cannot explain to better advantage the cultivation of trees; if that which precedes is well understood, one will be convinced that it is possible to acclimate these precious plants.

FLOWERS

➤-⊶-○-⊶-◄

If the plants of which I have spoken up to now are interesting for their utility, flowers also deserve the attention of the gardening enthusiast. They are the most beautiful ornament of the garden, and add an infinite value to the country life, both from the variety of the colors and from the sweetness of the fragrances that nearly all emit. The cultivation of flowers is one of the principal branches of the art of the gardener, and the most difficult. Since the limited extent of this work does not permit me to consider all of its developments, I will stick to putting as clearly as possible the general principles of this culture, according to which any intelligent person can cultivate his parterre, even raise exotic plants, and enjoy one of the sweetest pleasures that the science of cultivation can produce.

I pray my readers to remember the instructions on sowing seeds, which I gave [earlier]; this is a fundamental principle of the cultivation of flowers.

Since plants that are native or acclimated to the country do not offer any difficulties in cultivation, it suffices to raise the plants as the preceding article has said and to place them symmetrically in flower beds or in a parterre, varying the colors and arranging the plants in order according to their natural size and succession [of blooming], putting the largest somewhat far apart in order to put those that do not get as big in the interim spaces, and to provide in all parts of the planting for flowers that succeed one another, so that one does not see one end of the flower bed become bare, while the other is covered with blossoms.

Annuals are all sown in the springtime, as one can see in the gardener's almanac.

I am providing here a small nomenclature, giving the ordinary height of the stems and the color of the flowers. Varieties are indicated by the colors that distinguish them.

I am also indicating the time of flowering in temperate countries; one should expect some differences below this climate, which will not be very noticeable, however, since all must submit to the same influences.

By means of these instructions, one can manage one's planting as symmetrically as possible.

NOMENCLATURE AND CULTIVATION OF FLOWERS

Summer Adonis [Fr. *Adonis d'été;* Lat. *Adonis aestivalis* L.]—Stems one foot; flowers in June, bright red; sow in place, in light soil.

—

Fall Adonis [Fr. *Adonis d'automne;* Lat. *Adonis autumnalis* L.]—Same growing habit, same cultivation.

—

Amaranthus [Fr. *Amaranthe* or *amarante;* Lat. *Amaranthus caudatus* L.]—Stem 3 feet; flowers crimson, in a tail, which is why it is called foxtail, from June to September. Sow to transplant; all soils suit it. This has a variety with yellow flowers.

—

Tricolored amaranthus (Joseph's coat) [Fr. *Amaranthe tricolore;* Lat. *Amaranthus tricolor* L.]—Large leaves, touched with yellow, green and red. From June to September, green flowers.

—

Giant amaranthus [Fr. *Amaranthe gigantesque;* Lat. *Amaranthus speciosus* Ker.]—Stem 5 feet; flowers purple-crimson; sow in place, in March or April.

—

Hollyhock (rose mallow) [Fr. *Alcée, rose tremière,* or *passe-rose;* Lat. *Alcea rosea* L., Cavanilles]—Stems 8 feet; flowers from July to September. Numerous varieties; takes all colors, from white to dark yellow or to brownish crimson. Sow in a good exposure in September to transplant in March or April; protect from cold during the winter.

—

French hollyhock (Chinese althea), biennial [Fr. A*lcée de la Chine, bisannuelle;* Lat. *Alcea rosea sinensis* H.P.]—Stems 3 or 4 feet; flowers variegated with white and purple, from July to October. [A] variety with red flowers. If this is sown in hotbeds in February, it will flower the same year.

—

Amomum (false pepper) [Fr. *Amomum, faux piment;* Lat. *Solanum pseudo-capsicum* L.]—Stems from 3 to 4 feet; white flowers, from June to September; berries similar to little cherries, green at first, changing to yellow or to red, remaining all winter. Sow in hotbed in February, water frequently during the summer, little or not at all in the winter.

—

Columbine (aquilega), perennial [Fr. *Ancolie des jardins, vivace;* Lat. *Aquilegia vulgaris* L.]—Stem 3 feet; which divides into several branches. Flowers in May or June, pendant, red, blue, violet, white or pink, according to the variety; not at all difficult with soil, needs shade, averse to too much moisture. Sow the seeds as soon as they are ripe, or plant root divisions in spring or fall.

—

Garden anemone (windflower, broad-leaved anemone) [Fr. *Anémone des jardins;* Lat. *Anemone hortensis* L.]—Numerous varieties of different colors, flowers in May and June; buds swelling to 2 to 3 inches wide. The seed can be sown in this climate in autumn, the bulbs being planted in spring. This plant needs plenty of care, and a practiced hand to succeed well. Light, sweet, rich, and fresh soil; sandy soil fertilized with leaf mold is the kind that suits it best; sift it through a sieve or screen. If you plant seeds, do so in summer. The soil must be quite even; the seed spread on it must be covered with a layer of well-screened compost. Water lightly and weed carefully to keep the plant from being obstructed by weeds. Cover and water little in winter.

—

Garden balsam [Fr. *Balsamine;* Lat. *Impatiens balsamina* L.]—Fat stem, 2 feet high; flowers, varied according to the variety, sown in the springtime to be transplanted into flower beds.

—

Cornflower (bluebottle) [Fr. *Barbeau, espèce de centaurée;* Lat. *Centaurea cyanus* L.]—Several are grown which differ only in color.

Sow in place in February, in light soil, in the sun; one can sow from fall on by covering during the winter; transplant early to enjoy flowers in the spring. This plant must always be moved in a clump when transplanting.

—

Basil [Fr. *Basilic;* Lat. *Ocymum basilicum* L.]—Aromatic plant, known as *little balm.* Stem one foot; white or purplish flowers; sown in February in hotbeds to be transplanted in a clump, into flower beds or pots. There is a species with large leaves, well liked.[10]

—

Dwarf morning glory (bindweed) [Fr. *Belle de jour, liseron tricolore;* Lat. *Convolvulus tricolor* L.]—Stem one foot; flowers from June to September, varied from white to yellow and blue. Sow in place in April, or in hotbeds in February.

—

Four o'clock [Fr. *Belle de nuit;* Lat. *Mirabilis jalappa* L.]—Stems 2 feet; numerous flowers in bouquet; red, yellow, white or variegated; open only at night. Light, rich soil. Sow in spring.

—

Centaurea (mountain bluet) [Fr. *Bluet;* Lat. *Centaurea cyanus* L.]—This is [the same as] blue cornflower. See cornflower.

—

Celosia (cockscomb) [Fr. *Célosie, crête de coq;* Lat. *Celosia cristata* L.]—Stems 2 feet; small, numerous, serrated flowers, in long heads, flattened into a crest; red, yellow, or crimson, etc., according to the variety; sow in April in good soil or in March in hotbeds; transplant in clumps. This is averse to cold.

—

Emilia [Fr. *Cacalie odorante;* Lat. *Cacalia suaveolens* L.]—Numerous 4-foot stems; flowers from July to September; white, not very bright; with a pleasant aroma, balanced soil; propagated by seed or divisions. This is a perennial.

—

Spear-shaped cacalia [Fr. *Cacalia à feuilles hastées;* Lat. *Cacalia sagittata* W., *Emilia flammea sagittata, Cacalia coccinea*]—Stems 15 inches, somewhat branched, from July to September, red-orange flowers, very pretty. Sow in hotbeds in February for transplanting, or in place in April. There are a great number of varieties.[11]

—

Cactus [Fr. *Cactus;* Lat. *Cacti,* L.]—This family is very numerous. A great number of species are sought after because of their dazzlingly beautiful flowers. In several regions of Mexico the cochineal cactus is cultivated for instruction in *cochenille,* so useful in the art of coloring.

Cacti are propagated by cuttings from crowns or split-off leaves, of which the cut has been allowed to dry before being put into the ground. One can graft them one onto another, thus making bizarre combinations. This operation cannot be executed except by a practiced hand.

—

Garden campanula (bellflower), perennial [Fr. *Campanule des jardins, vivace;* Lat. *Campanula persicifolia* L.]—Stems 18 inches; from June to September, large, successive, bell-shaped flowers, white or blue; light soil, propagated by divisions or by seed sown as soon as they mature without being covered.

—

Chimney bellflower [Fr. *Campanule pyramidale, bisannuelle;* Lat. *Campanula pyramidalis* L.]—Stem 4 to 5 feet; from July to September, beautiful blue flowers, growing in clusters and bouquets; there is [also] a variety with white flowers. Light soil, frequent watering.

—

Canterbury bells and Venus's looking-glass [Fr. *Campanule à grosse fleurs* and *campanule doucette (miroir de Vénus);* Lat. *Campanula medium* L. and *Campanula speculum/Specularia speculum-veneris* L.]—Violet flowers.

—

Our Lady's glove [Fr.. *Campanule gantelée, campanule dorée,* etc.; Lat. *Campanula trachelium* L. and *Campanula aurea* L.]—Same cultivation for all varieties.

—

Nasturtium, annual [Fr. *Capuchine;* Lat. *Tropaeolum majus* L.]— Creeping stem. Flowers during the entire summer, yellow-orange.

—

Nasturtium, crimson, red. [Fr. *Capucine pourpre, rouge;* Lat. *Tropaeolum majus* var.]—Sow in the spring, in place; support the branches by stakes or attach them along a wall.

—

Honeysuckle [Fr. *Chèvrefeuille;* Lat. *Lonicera capriifolium* L.]—Flexible stem, more or less tall according to the species; flowers varying from tender pink to red; propagated by cuttings, layering, or seeds.

This family is numerous,[12] [and] several species are good for bedecking arbors. Their aroma is very sweet, [and] their thick foliage provides shade. There are, however, several dwarf species, which can serve to ornament the middle of flower beds.

—

Garden chrysanthemum [Fr. *Chrysanthème des jardins;* Lat. *Chrysanthemum coronarium* L.]—Stem 2 feet; from July to September, white or yellow flowers. Sow in all soils, but better in balanced soil.

—

Tricolor chrysanthemum [Fr. *Chrysanthème caréné;* Lat. *Chrysanthemum carinatum* Sch.]—Stems one foot; large flowers with brown disks and white rays, but yellow at the base, opening in the sun and closing outside as soon as it goes down.

Several other species are cultivated; the culture is nearly the same for all.

—

Dusty miller (rose campion) [Fr. *Coquelourde des jardins;* Lat. *Agrostemma coronaria* L.]—Stem 18 inches, whitish; from June to September, numerous, white, scarlet, or reddish-purple flowers; in the form of a little eye; plant the seed or divide the roots.

—

Jupiter flower (lychnis, flower of Jove), perennial [Fr. *Coquelourde, fleur de Jupiter;* Lat. *Agrostemma flos-jovis* L.]—Purplish flowers; same cultivation, divisions in March. Another variety with pink flowers is grown.[13]

—

Dahlia (numerous genera)[14] [Fr. *Dahlia;* Lat. *Dahlia*]—Tall stems, covered with magnificent rayed flowers, with infinitely varied colors. Propagated by seed sown in a good exposure in March, and in well-composted earth; from tubers transplanted in spring; by cuttings made in May, planted in hotbeds; keep it from getting air until it takes root.

—

Hyacinth bean [Fr. *Dolique;* Lat. *Dolichos lablab*]—Resembling green beans with which they are frequently confused. Several varieties are perfect for decorating arbors, which they cover with thick foliage. Different colored flowers during the entire summer and fall, very numerous, ordinarily growing in clusters. One red-flowered species[15] is grown in this country, [which] produces a most beautiful effect. Sow in February, and up until May, in rows and in place.

—

Eglantine (wild rose, dog rose, sweetbrier) [Fr. *Eglantier, rosier sauvage;* Lat. *Rosa rubiginosa*]—Serves as a stock for grafting all kinds of roses. This can be sown from seed; its cultivation is easy.

—

Passionflower (yellow granidilla, water lemon, jamaica honeysuckle) [Fr. *Fleurs de la passion, grenadille;* Lat. *Passiflora laurifolia* L.]—Stems 10 to 11 feet; large and beautiful flowers, pleasantly varied in color, to which succeed fruit as big as an egg, with a delicate taste. Sow in mellow soil, along a wall, on an arbor, or on a fence; its root is perennial.

A dozen species are known, all sought for the happy disposition of their flowers.

—

Geranium [Fr. *Géranier, géranium;* Lat. *Pelargonium* L'Her.]—More than 300 species of this family are cultivated. They can be sown from seed, but the seed rarely reproduces the true species, which is why cuttings are preferred, from July to September, in tamped soil, three weeks sufficing for them to make their roots.

Since the plants do not grow tall and are averse to frost, they are put in pots to be brought inside during winter.

—

Wallflower [Fr. *Giroflée;* Lat. *Cheiranthus cheiri* L.]—Bushy plant, 1 to 2 feet; numerous flowers, white, yellow, violet, pink, red, crimson, etc., according to the species. Sow in March in a raised hotbed, water little, transplant into the nursery or into place. Some people out of curiosity graft wallflowers onto cabbage, with which they are congenerous. One can also graft branches of various species onto the same base, the colors mixing together will produce a very nice effect. This succeeds well through cuttings.

—

Wallflower quarantaine [Fr. *Giroflée quarantaine;* Lat. *Cheiranthus annuus* L.]—Less bushy stem, forming tufts of attractive flowers; same culture.

—

Virginian stock (Mahon's wallflower) [Fr. *Giroflée de Mahon;* Lat. *Cheiranthus maritimus* L.]—Small border plant, covered with flowers in spring. Sow in rows in place.

—

Ice plant [Fr. *Glacial;* Lat. *Mesembryanthemum crystallinum* L.]— Stem 2 feet, plump and fleshy, succulent leaves; in July and August, little white flowers. The whole plant, except for the flower, is full of transparent cells full of water, which make it appear as if covered with ice; the hotter it gets the more the cells multiply. Sow in hotbeds; transplant into a full exposure.

—

Pomegranate [Fr. *Grenadier;* Lat. *Punica granatum*]—Pomegranates root by cuttings in ligature. Propagation is easier through sprouts which grow frequently from the roots.

—

Heliotrope [Fr. *Héliotrope;* Lat. *Heliotropium peruvianum*]—Small shrub of 2 to 3 feet. From June until November, small bluish flowers with the aroma of vanilla. Light, balanced soil, frequent waterings in summer. Seeds or cuttings in hotbeds, in the spring and in summer. Protect it from cold in winter.

—

Hydrangea [Fr. *Hortensia;* Lat. *Hydrangea macrophylla, H. hortensia* Smith]—Handsome shrub of 3 to 4 feet; from June until November, flowers in balls of a purplish red, then violet-like, finally a soiled white, and sometimes a bright red. Cuttings in springtime, [in] peat moss, refreshed frequently, lots of water during the summer. Bring it in during winter.

Blue flowers are obtained by planting in soil high in iron.

—

Everlasting (strawflower, immortelle, helichrysum) [Fr. *Immortelle;* Lat. *Gnaphalium foétidum* L.]—Stems 1 to 2 feet. Flowers in bouquet, large, white, yellow, etc., calyx silvery. Surviving well over several years when they are cut fresh and dried upside down. Propagated by seed in the springtime, or by cuttings in summer, in the shade.

—

Jasmine [Fr. *Jasmin;* Lat. *Jasminum*]—Many species are grown,[16] all rooting by cuttings, better by layers bedded in fall.

—

Hibiscus [Fr. *Hibiscus;* Lat. *Hibiscus*]—Stems 4 feet; flowers in August, large, sulphur yellow, purple in the center. Light soil, sown in the springtime.[17] Several species are grown and make a pleasing effect from their large flowers and happy disposition. There are some with white, purple, pink, rose, etc. flowers. Hibiscus are averse to cold, and often die back in winter; sheltered, they sprout again in the spring.

—

Oleander [Fr. *Laurier rose;* Lat. *Nerium* L.]—Charming shrub, forming clumps with flexible wood 2 to 4 feet high; light to dark pink flowers. Propagated in light soil by seed, cuttings, layers, or grafts. A large number of species and varieties are grown.

—

Lavender [Fr. *Lavande;* Lat. *Lavandula spica* L.]—Shrub of 2 feet; bluish flowers, in whorled spikes. Several species with red, violet,[18] dark blue,[19] etc. flowers. The first one is cultivated for the aroma of the leaves and flowers. Sow in hotbeds; transplant into light soil, in the middle of the flower bed.

—

Lily [Fr. *Lis;* Lat. *Lilium candidum* L.]—Stems 3 to 4 feet; flowers white, varied, variegated, etc., according to the species. Since lilies are planted by bulbs, they can be shipped to remote places, but they succeed better when replanted in the ground right away, five inches deep.

—

Martagon (Turk's cap lily) [Fr. *Lis martagon;* Lat. *Lilium martagon* L.]—In July, purple flowers; stems not so high, pleasant aroma; averse to frost.

This very numerous genus [i.e., lilies] produces some magnificent flowers.

—

Convolvulacea family [Fr. *Famille des liserons;* Lat. *Convolvulaceæ*]—Numerous genus of which most of the species have slender, climbing stems, decorating arbors with their tendrils and the variety of their flowers. Sow in the spring in any soil.

—

Snapdragon [Fr. *Mufflier, muffle de veau* or *guele de lion* (literally "calf's nose" or "lion's snout"); Lat. *Antirrhinun majus* L.]—Stem 2 to 3 feet; in May and August, spiked flowers, like a snout, red, white, purple, etc., according to the variety. Propagated by seed or by cuttings.

—

Lily of the valley [Fr. *Muguet;* Lat. *Convallaria maialis* L.]—Small perennial plant with runner roots. Stem 6 inches; white flowers shaped like small bells, in May; [a] variety with light red flowers,[20] and one with double flowers;[21] all have a very agreeable aroma.

Any soil, but cool and shaded; [propagate by] shoots, root cuttings, or seeds sown in place.

—

Myrtle [Fr. *Myrte;* Lat. *Myrtus communnis*]—Shrubs of which several species are grown because of their handsome evergreen foliage, and for their attractive shape.

Myrtles love a friable, light soil, [and] plenty of water and sun; disliking frost. Seeds, layers, or cuttings.

—

Narcissus (daffodil) [Fr. *Narcisse, porion;* Lat. *Narcissus poeticus* L.]— Stem one foot; in May, white flower, fragrant, with a crown bordered with purple; several varieties.[22]

Plant the bulbs in October, water.

—

Dianthus (pinks) [Fr. *Oeillet* (literally "eye"); Lat. *Dianthus caryophyllus* L.]—Stems from 18 to 30 inches; from July to August, flowers in several colors, simple, semidouble, or double according to the variety, with the aroma of wallflower.

Gardeners have made infinite varieties of this genus. Pinks are propagated by seeds, layers, or cuttings in good soil, in the shade. To layer them, you must suspend watering for the preceding two or three days so that the stems, withering, become more flexible and lend themselves to bending over without breaking. This operation must be performed when the flowers begin to fade. The stems being weak, they must be supported with stakes to which they are tied.

On high land, one can grow pinks in the open ground, but in humid soils one has to put them in pots or in boxes 6 to 8 inches in diameter, full of good, mellow, well-composted soil. They are kept in the open from the month of April until the month of October or later if warm weather persists, and in a dry and aerated place during the winter. Layers made in July or August must not be cut until the following spring, and should be pulled up in clumps for replanting.

In addition to this care, the pink needs to have all of its dead leaves removed [and] the collar cleaned of anything that might cause rotting, to which this plant is very susceptible.

Some gardeners practice a very good method, which they call cone layering. They take sheet metal, of the thickness of a card, which they cut into a triangle and roll into the shape of a cone around the branch of the pink they want to layer, having previously made an incision on the branch as far as the pith, beveled in a clear spot on the underside. They attach the cone at the level required by the height of the branch, on pickets inserted into the ground, [and] fill the horn with good soil, which must be maintained slightly moist. In spring they cut off the layer and plant it in a clump.

—

African marigold [Fr. *Oeillet d'Inde, tagétès élevé;* Lat. *Tagetes erecta* L.]—Straight stem with a height 2 to 3 feet. Large, solitaire, and yellow flowers from July to October; strong and disagreeable odor. Sow in hotbeds, transplant; numerous waterings.

—

Auricula [Fr. *Oreille d'ours* (literally "bear's-ear"); Lat. *Primula auricula*]—See bear's-ear *(Primavère, oreille d'ours).*

—

Hollyhock [Fr. *Passe-rose, alcée, rose tremière;* Lat. *Alcea rosea* L.]—Hardy triennial plant. Stem from 7 to 9 feet; from July to September, large, simple, semidouble, or double flowers, quite varied in color, from white to dark yellow, or to brownish crimson.

Sow in light, rich soil; transplant well apart; protect from frost by covering in winter.

—

Passionflower [Fr. *Passiflore;* Lat. *Passiflora* L.]—Climbing plants suitable for covering arbors or embellishing a fence. Numerous, magnificent flowers, giving rise to fruit with a taste more or less fine according to the variety. The pomegranate or false grenade is of this genus.

Propagated by seed, cuttings, layers and grafts. Light, soft, and rich soil.

—

Garden poppy [Fr. *Pavot des jardins;* Lat. *Papaver somniferum* L.]— Stem 3 to 4 feet; numerous varieties of all colors except blue, plain or variegated. Sow in place; all soils suit it.

—

Pansy [Fr. *Pensée, violette tricolore;* Lat. *Viola tricolor* L.]—Everyone knows this little plant, symbol of constant friendship. A large number of species are grown, among which we distinguish the tricolor, which has produced some superb varieties. Flowers from May until September. Sow in the springtime in the shade, or better replant old root divisions; mellow, light soil.

—

Periwinkle [Fr. *Pervenche;* Lat. *Vinca* L.]—Clumps with trailing or climbing branches, 2 to 4 feet; from May until September; white flowers, or pink, or tender blue, or red, according to the species.[23] Sow in hotbeds; replant into all soils. This is also propagated by shoots.

—

Larkspur (delphinium) [Fr. *Pied d'alouette, pyramidale;* Lat. *Delphinium ajacis* L.]—Stem 1 to 6 feet, according to the species, which are numerous. From June to August, flowers in spikes, simple, semi-double, or double; pink, red, or blue, sometimes white. Sow in balanced soil; cover with compost.

—

Poinciana [Fr. *Poinsillade, poinciana;* Lat. *Poinciana/Delonix regia?*]—Five- to ten-foot shrub, sprouting numerous stems from the stock; flowers in July, poppy red, in pyramidal clusters of the greatest elegance; [also a] variety with yellow flowers. Sow in hotbeds or propagate by cuttings. Shelter during the winter.

—

Primrose [Fr. *Primavère;* Lat. *Primula veris*]—Low perennial plant; spring flowering. Numerous varieties, of varying colors from orange to velvety brown. Sow in light, cool, and shaded soil; transplant in autumn, or make root divisions to perpetuate the pure species.

—

Bear's-ear (auricula) [Fr. *Primavère, oreille d'ours;* Lat. *Primula auricula, Primula alpina*]—Simple stem 3 to 6 inches high; flowers in umbels; from March until May, and frequently also in fall. Sow in hotbeds in December; transplant when the plant has 5 or 6 leaves, in very light soil. Several other species are grown, of which the cultivation is nearly the same.

—

Ranunculus (Persian buttercup) [Fr. *Renoncule;* Lat. *Ranunculus asiaticus* L.]—Claw consisting of several fingers, giving birth to a stem 6 to 18 inches high with a terminating flower. Sometimes the stem branches; numerous varieties offering all shades of color, except blue. They are simple, semidouble, or double. Sow seed to obtain different varieties, but to preserve a fine species, plant the claws in soil composed of one part loam, one of sand, and two of well-composted leaf mold. Sift the soil several times over, so that it is well broken up and filtered of stones or brick particles; [put] in pots or boxes, or even in flower beds in an eastern exposure, either in December, covering the plant during frosts, or as soon as they are no longer to be feared for. They must be planted 6 to 8 inches apart, in very straight and even lines, so that the leaves of the plant cover the earth entirely. When planting in the springtime, one must soak the claws for 12 hours in a concoction of soot, to drive away insects. Weed the plant carefully, water with a fine sprinkling in dry weather. Pull up the claws after the leaves dry, remove the leaves and stems, then put them into a screen and immerse in water. The soil will wash away and pass through the screen with the water. When they have withered, divide them and let them dry in the shade in order to store them in boxes or paper sacks. One can have ranunculus full of flowers in all seasons by planting every fortnight; they must be in pots in winter. The claws last more than a year out of the ground.

—

Reseda (mignonette) [Fr. *Réséda;* Lat. *Reseda odorata* L.]—Small decumbent plant; the extremities of the stems turning up. Greenish flowers with a very sweet aroma; all soils. By sowing the seed frequently one can enjoy it all year. Put in a pot in winter; do not transplant.

—

Castor bean (palma Christi) [Fr. *Ricin, palma-Christi;* Lat. *Ricinus communis* L.]—Stems to a height of 6 to 10 feet; in June or July, flowers in clusters, single, but beautiful, pleasantly varied. Light and rich soil. Sow in the spring in hotbeds or in a full exposure.

—

Rosemary [Fr. *Romarin;* Lat. *Rosmarinus officinalis* L.]—Shrub 2 to 5 feet high. Branches in whorls; from February to May, pale blue flowers in bouquets. Light soil; full exposure, propagated by root divisions, by cuttings, and by layers; one can also sow the seed; cover it if it freezes badly.

—

Hibiscus (Chinese hibiscus, rose of China, camellia) [Fr. *Rose de la Chine, ketmie;* Lat. *Hibiscus rosa-sinensis* L.]—Shrub 2 to 5 feet high, with much effect. Large flowers, either red or white, or yellow, or rosy gold; single or double, during the whole summer. Sow in hotbeds, or [make] cuttings also in hotbeds; cover in the winter.

Rose of China or of Japan is also called Camellia (Camellia Japonica). [A] superb shrub, evergreen, from 2 to 8 feet. Axillary and terminal flowers; the thick petals are either red or pink, or white, or variegated, like the most beautiful porcelain. Light soil, mixed with compost, part sun in summer, shelter in winter. Propagated by seed or by cuttings under bell glass, or finally by tie-layering.

—

Roses [Fr. *Rosier;* Lat. *Rosa*]—Describing the rose would be superfluous; the whole world recognizes it as the queen of flowers, and the symbol of freshness and beauty.

The most beautiful as well as the easiest to cultivate is the centifolia; nevertheless, we will leave it for varieties less beautiful, but which have the merit of novelty. China roses have enjoyed and still enjoy success merited by their variety and color and the elegance of their forms; nevertheless, one is always forced to return to the type of beautiful species when one wants to express the idea of the sweet aroma belonging to the genus, and the fineness of the coloration. The extent of this work does not allow for giving the nomenclature of its varieties or subvarieties, numbering more than 2000. I will limit myself to pointing out the method of cultivation. [Garden] enthusiasts who want to create new varieties can achieve this through seeds in light soil improved with compost; sow the seeds as soon as they are ripe; cover the seedbeds during cold weather. If one sows in the spring, one must soak the seed in water for 24 hours; several seeds will come up in the spring, the others the following year. The young plant is given the same care as the seed[lings] of other plants.

To preserve pure species, it is necessary to plant shoots, or make layers.

Roses are grafted on the eglantine or wild rose, several kinds succeeding on the Bengal [Chinese] rose.

Roses are pruned in spring, in the first days of March, or sooner if the [warm] season is early. Suppress all dead or diseased branches, or those that might be advantageously replaced, either by another already existing or by those promised by buds. Finally, shorten last year's shoots to 1 or 2 eyes in order to get large flowers; several species need nothing more than to be cleaned of dead or diseased wood.

—

Scabiosa (pincushion flower) [Fr. *Scabieuse, fleur de veuve;* Lat. *Scabiosa atropurpurea* L.]—Stem 2 feet; from July to October, flowers of a more or less dark, velvety purple, pink or variegated; musk aroma, or of *fourmi.* Balanced, light soil. Sow in the springtime; better in fall in place; a covering [is needed] in winter.

—

Groundsel (purple ragwort) [Fr. *Seneçon d'Espagne;* Lat. *Senecio elegans* L.]—Straight stem 12 to 15 inches high, sometimes branched; flowers radiating in rays, a clear and superb crimson, disk a beautiful golden yellow, from June to August; varieties with different colors. Sow in March in sweet and well-composted earth; transplant into rows to be strengthened, finally put into place where it will flower in fall. Well treated, it can endure for 3 years.

—

Sensitive plant [Fr. *Sensitive* or *acacie pudique;* Lat. *Mimosa pudica*]—This plant is sought by [garden] enthusiasts because of its great sensitivity. At the least touch the leaves close up and the petals wither. Stems 2 feet, armed with hooked needles. In summer, flowers of a red violet, very small, forming light tufts. Plant one seed in each pot to avoid transplanting, depot to put in place, in light composted soil; cover in winter.

—

Mock orange [Fr. *Seringa odorant;*[24] Lat. *Philadelphus coronarius* L.]—Shrub forming a bush 8 to 10 feet high; in June, white flowers, with an agreeable aroma, but strong. Grows in all soils and in any exposure; cuttings, layers, shoots, or division.

—

Sunflower [Fr. *Soleil, tournesol* (literally "turn toward the sun"); Lat. *Helianthus annuus* L.]—Stem 4 to 6 feet; flowers with yellow center and rays, 4 to 7 inches wide, single or double, propagated by seed, in hotbeds; transplant far apart. Varieties with red flowers and small flowers.

—

Marigold [Fr. *Souci commun;* Lat. *Calendula officinalis*]—Low stem; flowers saffron yellow; sow in mellow, rich soil; transplant into flower beds. Numerous species, with lighter or darker flowers; several of them are averse to cold.

—

African marigold [Fr. *Tagetes;* Lat. *Tagetes erecta* L.]—This is the same thing as Indian pink [*oeillet d'Inde*].

—

Candytuft [Fr. *Thlaspi;* Lat. *Iberis semperflorens* L.]—Small perennial plant, forming thick clumps full of very white flowers in corymbs, from October to March; light soil, shelter during winter, propagation by seeds or cuttings.

—

Edging candytuft [Fr. *Thlaspi à bordures;* Lat. *Iberis sempervirens* L.]—Smaller than the preceding.

—

Globe candytuft [Fr. *Thlaspi en ombelles;* Lat. *Iberis umbellata* L.]— Stems one foot high; in July, white flowers or in a pretty violet; likes to be transplanted in clumps.

—

Candytuft julienne [Fr. *Thlaspi julienne;* Lat. ?][25]—Flowers in long clusters with a beautiful effect; same cultivation.

—

Tuberose [Fr. *Tubéreuse, oignon brun allongé;* Lat. *Polyanthes tuberosa* L.]—Stem 3 to 5 feet. White flowers bathed with pink, in spikes; very sweet and penetrating aroma. Single, semidouble, or double flowers according to the variety. Plant in March in light and rich soil, cover in cold weather; water copiously in dry weather. The bulbs do not flower until the third year.

—

Tulip (long bulb) [Fr. *Tulipe, oignon allongé;* Lat. *Tulipa sylvestris* L.]—Stems 6 to 18 inches according to the species. Different colored flowers from yellow to crimson, frequently variegated. Bulbs and corms planted in November in good soil, or seeds in October in soft, rich earth; the corms must not be pulled up from the seedbeds until the second year.

The varieties of tulips are infinite. Together they all create a beautiful effect by the elegance of their bearing and the variety of their colors. This genus has been more sought after in former times than the dahlia is today.

—

Verbena [Fr. *Vervein;* Lat. *Lippia, Verbena*]—A somewhat numerous genus,[26] of which several kinds grow spontaneously in this country. There are some with pink flowers, with blue flowers, purple, white, etc. These plants, neglected because they are seen everywhere, are very effective in the garden, and require no care.[27]

—

Violet [Fr. *Violette odorante;* Lat. *Viola odorata* L.]—[A] small plant, hiding under hedges and in the woods, which is why it is chosen for the symbol of modesty. [Having] the sweetest aroma, [and] flowers in the springtime, of white or blue, or variegated with red and violet, most often violet, as the name of the plant suggests.

Sow in leaf mold, or separate the old feet in soft earth, somewhat shaded; cover with straw matting or with stable litter in winter, to make it flower early. The four-seasons violet[28] flowers from September until March, and flowers again in various seasons.

—

Stock (wallflower) [Fr. *Violier;* Lat. *Cheiranthus cheiri* L.]—This is the same thing as wallflower.

—

Red zinnia [Fr. *Zinnia, zinnia rouge, bresine;* Lat. *Zinnia multiflora* L.]—Stems 18 inches to 2 feet; from July to October, numerous flowers having yellow disks with bright red rays, which it maintains until the seeds mature, which self-sow frequently.[29]

—

Zinnia (pink-flowering, bright-red-flowering, etc.) [Fr. *Zinnia à fleurs roses, à fleurs rouge-vif, etc.;* Lat. *Zinnia elegans* Jacq.]—Sow in the springtime in hotbeds; transplant into rows to strengthen the plant; then replant in clumps, in light, rich soil.

—

The plants named above may be cultivated somewhat easily, requiring only the ordinary care recommended. Exotic plants, above all those from hot regions, demand more care; they like to be potted and brought inside in winter, in a warm and well-lighted place, sometimes in a hothouse.

I have not spoken at all about some plants that are well acclimated in this country, and of which everyone is familiar with the cultivation; for the rest, the procedures indicated above are applicable to all species of plants, except for some modifications according to their nature and growing habits.

I have indicated several herbaceous plants that can be propagated by grafts; but since this operation differs from that used for ligneous [woody] plants, I will now describe it.

HERBACEOUS GRAFTING

Choose a branch with a good terminal eye from the plant to be propagated. Trim the graft like the blade of a knife, then making a long slit on the stock, either on a bare spot, [or] better at a leaf axil, insert the graft there, [and] make a ligature to join the parts. You must shield the grafts from the rays of the sun while they are new, and after several days suppress the buds below the graft. When you are sure it has taken, loosen the ligature a little bit, and cut off the leaf which might draw the sap toward the graft, but which may, at this point, turn it to its exclusive benefit.

To assure the success of these kinds of grafts, one must observe: that the cut of the graft be made with a very sharp instrument, without wounding the fibers; that the slit made on the stock be quite perpendicular, and that it separate the fibers from the bark and wood without cutting their threads, as much as that is possible, so that the sap-filled cells are well aligned and the nourishing juices pass easily from the stock into the scion.

This operation does not present great difficulties; it suffices to practice several times to do it with success. By this process one can produce different-colored wallflowers on a cabbage stock, a cucumber base will grow pumpkins, and a dahlia of mediocre but vigorous quality can be covered with magnificent flowers, etc., etc.

This graft can also be applied to trees. It is useful above all for resinous trees, but one must always practice it when the stock is young.

APPENDIX
CALENDAR ITEMS

➤─┤─◆➤─○─◆─┤─◄

✦ THE YEAR ✦

The calendar year is regulated by the movement of the sun; it differs from the lunar year by about 11 days.

The solar or calendar year is a little more than 365 and one-fourth days, which is the time that the sun takes to make an orbit from the west to the east. We ignore the quarter day for three consecutive years, which are the ordinary years; they have only 365 days; but we count 366 days in the fourth year to make up for the neglected quarter days. This year is called leap year.

The year is divided into four seasons:

Spring, which begins on the 21st of March; summer, which begins the 22nd of June; autumn, which begins the 23rd of September; and winter, which begins on the 22nd of December.

The time of the beginning of each season is called the equinox.

The lunar year has only about 354 and a third days; it is composed of 12 lunar months, which are counted from one new moon to the other.

Each lunation or lunar month is a little more than 29 and one-half days; this is why we count them alternately from 30 to 29 days.

Pages 9–23 of the French text deal with astronomical concepts important to the nineteenth-century French gardener. These include calculating the phases of the moon; finding the "golden number," the "epact," and the "dominical letter"; and knowing the

We say that the moon is new when it rises with the sun; then we do not see it; and that it is full when it rises at the moment that the sun sets; then its disk is round. These two periods are called syzygies.

The solar months are counted alternately as 31 and 30 days, except for February, which has only 28 days in ordinary years, and 29 in leap years.

When the month has 31 days the moon has 30, and if it has only 30 days, the moon has only 29.

The phases of the moon are of interest to the grower because of the changes that they often bring in the state of the atmosphere, and which is good to foresee, to arrange his work schedule.

To calculate the phases of the moon, we consider the golden number and the epacts.

⟶ THE GOLDEN NUMBER ⟵

The golden number is a cycle of 19 years, at the end of which the new and full moons return on the same days of the month and at nearly the same hour [that they did at the beginning of the cycle], since at the end of 19 years the like phases advance only 1 hour 28 minutes. The golden number serves to find the epact, which is used to calculate the phases of the moon.

The golden number increases by one each year, and when the cycle of 19 is finished we begin again to count at one. To find it, for any year whatsoever of the Christian era, one must add one to the date of the proposed year, and divide the sum by 19; the remainder of the division (disregarding the quotient) is the sought-for golden number. If there is no remainder, the golden number is 19. One adds 1 to the proposed

---

saints' feast days. We have elected to remove these sections from their original place and present them here as an appendix.—Tr.

year before doing the division because the golden number was one in the [year of] the birth of J[esus] C[hrist].

Suppose we want to find the golden number for the year 1842: adding 1 we will get 1843; dividing by 19, the remainder will be 0; thus, the golden number will be 19; but if we are looking for that of the year 1855, operating as above we will have for the remainder, and for the golden number, 13.

✦ THE EPACT ✦

Epacts are numbers that express, for each year, the phase, nearly, of the moon, at the end of the preceding year. This number corresponds also to the phase of the moon on the last day of February of the current year.

To find the epact of any year whatever between 1700 and 1900 exclusively, subtract 1 from the golden number of that year and multiply the remainder by 11, then divide the product by 30; what remains after the division is the epact for that year.

To ascertain the date for the new moon in any month whatever in a given year, from March to December inclusively, add the number of months gone by to the number of the epact, counting March as the first, up to and including the month for which one seeks the new moon. This sum will diminish by a lunation, that is to say, by 29 or 30 days, according to whether the month has 30 or 31 days; the remainder gives the day of the month when the new moon will appear. If the sum of the months and the epact should be greater than 29 or 30, one would have to go back 59 days, the amount of 2 lunar months.

For the months of January and February one has only to add 1 to the epact of the proposed year, and take away the sum of 30 for January and 29 for February.

To find out on which day the full moon falls in the same month, add

15 to the date of the new moon if it arrives before the 15th, or subtract that amount if it arrives later. I will clarify this with an example:

Suppose that we want to find the days of the new and full moons in May 1838; suppose also that we know neither the golden number nor the epact of that year.

Adding 1 to 1838 we have 1839, which we divide by 19; the remainder 15 will indicate the golden number. Subtracting 1 from the golden number 15 and multiplying the remainder 14 by 11, the product will be 154, which, divided by 30, gives a remainder of 4 for the epact of 1838. If to the number 4 of the epact, we add the number 3 for the months that have elapsed from March to May inclusively, we will have 7; reducing this sum by 30, because May has 31 days, the remainder 23 indicates that the new moon will be on the 23rd of May; subtracting 15 from the 23rd we will get 8 for the date of the full moon. Therefore, the 8th of May will have a full moon, and the 23rd will have a new moon. These calculations are not exact; they may err by 2 days, but they are sufficient to guide the grower on the variations that might come on with the changes of the syzygies.

✦ THE DOMINICAL LETTER ✦

The dominical letter serves to identify Sundays. It changes every year on the 1st of January; leap years have two; the first serves for January and February, the second for the rest of the year.

✦ MOVABLE FEASTS ✦

Movable feasts are all regulated by the feast of Easter. Easter is fixed on the closest Sunday to the full moon originating in March. To avoid calculations that may be fatiguing, I am providing a table of time [years] and of movable feasts. One will find there the dominical letters for each year, by means of which one can make longer use of the following calendar.

TABLE OF SEASONS AND MOVABLE FEASTS

Year	Epact	Dominical Letter	Septuagesima	Ash Wednesday	Easter	Pentecost	Advent Sunday
1838	VI	g	February 11	February 28	April 1	June 3	December 2
1839	XV	f	January 27	February 13	March 31	May 19	December 1
1840	XXVI	e, d	February 16	March 4	April 19	June 7	November 29
1841	VII	c	February 7	February 24	April 11	May 30	November 28
1842	XVIII	b	January 23	February 9	March 27	May 17	November 27
1843	XVIII	A	February 12	March 1	April 16	June 4	December 3
1844	XI	g, f	February 4	February 21	April 7	May 26	December 1
1845	XXII	e	January 19	February 5	March 23	May 11	November 30
1846	III	d	February 8	February 25	April 12	May 31	November 29
1847	XIV	c	January 31	February 17	April 4	May 23	November 28

By means of this table and of the instructions that precede it, the following calendar can substitute for an ordinary almanac until one is obtained. This is why I used the dominical letter to indicate the days of the week; one will recall that the year's letter indicates Sunday; so, during 1838, the dominical letter being *g,* all the days that correspond to *g* will be Sundays, and the other letters will indicate the other days of the week. The year 1840 has two dominical letters: *e, d;* the first, *e,* will serve for January and February, but it will change on the first of March, because of the 29th day of February in leap years. So *d* will indicate Sundays for the rest of the year, beginning with and including March.

Appendix

		JANUARY			FEBRUARY

JANUARY

The Month has 31 *days
and the Moon* 30.

FEBRUARY

The Month has 28 *days
and the Moon* 29.

1	A	THE CIRCUMCISION	1	d	Ignatius m[artyr]
2	b	Macarius	2	e	Purification
3	c	Genevieve	3	f	Blaise
4	d	Benedict	4	g	Andrew *Cors.*
5	e	Simeon	5	A	Agatha
6	f	Kings' Day	6	b	Dorothy
7	g	Lucius	7	c	Romwald
8	A	John *Calib.*	8	d	John of *Mat.*
9	b	Julian	9	e	Appolinus
10	c	William	10	f	Scholastica
11	d	Hyginus	11	g	*Saturnin*
12	e	Arcadius	12	A	Eulalie
13	f	Leonce	13	b	Benignus
14	g	Hilary, bishop	14	c	Valentine
15	A	Maurice, abbot	15	d	Faustinus
16	b	Marcel	16	e	*Onésime*
17	c	Anthony, abbot	17	f	*Théodule*
18	d	Ch[arles?] St. Peter	18	g	Simon
19	e	Canut, bishop	19	A	Conrad
20	f	Fabian and Sebastian	20	b	Eucherius
21	g	Agnes	21	c	Fortune
22	A	Vincent, D[eacon?]	22	d	Ch[arles?] St. Peter[?] *A.*
23	b	Emerentiana	23	e	*Florent*
24	c	Timothy	24	f	Matthias
25	d	Conversion of St. Paul	25	g	*Claudien*
26	e	Polycarp	26	A	Alexander
27	f	John Chrysostom	27	b	Leander
28	g	Ildephonsus	28	c	Theophilus
29	A	Martin			
30	b	Francis de Sales			*In leap year, this month*
31	c	Peter *Nol.*			*has 29 d.*

Appendix

	MARCH			APRIL	
	*The Month has 31 days and the Moon 30.*			*The Month has 30 days and the Moon 29.*	
1	d	*Aubin* [Aubignac?]	1	g	Hugh
2	e	*Simplice*	2	A	Francis the *P.*
3	f	Cunegunda	3	b	Richard
4	g	Casimir	4	c	Isidore
5	A	Drausin, bishop	5	d	Vincent *F.*
6	b	Victor	6	e	Celestine
7	c	Thomas Aquinas	7	f	*Egésipe*
8	d	John of God	8	g	Dionis
9	e	Frances	9	A	Cleophus
10	f	40 Martyrs	10	b	*Macaire*
11	g	Candide	11	c	Leon, p[ope]
12	A	Paul, bishop	12	d	Victor, martyr
13	b	Euphrasie	13	e	Hermanigilda
14	c	Matilda	14	f	Tiburtius
15	d	Longinus	15	g	Anastasia
16	e	Abraham	16	A	Lambert
17	f	Patricia	17	b	*Anicet*
18	g	Gabriel	18	C	Perfect
19	A	Joseph	19	d	Timony *(Timon)*
20	b	*Cathebert*	20	e	Theodore
21	c	Benoit	21	f	Anselm
22	d	*Bazile* [Basil?]	22	g	Soter
23	e	Victoria	23	A	George
24	f	Simon, martyr	24	b	*Fidelise*
25	g	Annunciation	25	c	Mark
26	A	Felix, bishop	26	d	Cletus and Marcellinus
27	b	John, *h.* [hermit]	27	e	Frederick
28	c	*Gontran*	28	f	Vitalien
29	d	Eustacius	29	g	Peter, martyr
30	3	Amedee	30	A	Catherine de S[ales]
31	f	*Balbine*			

MAY			JUNE		
The Month has 31 *days and the Moon* 30.			*The Month has* 30 *days and the Moon* 29.		
1	b	James and Philip	1	e	Pamphilus
2	c	Athanasius	2	f	Marcelinus
3	d	Discovery of the Holy Cross	3	g	Clotilde
4	e	Monica	4	A	*Quirin*
5	f	Pius V, pope	5	b	Boniface
6	g	John *P. L.*	6	c	Norbert
7	A	Stanislaus	7	d	Robert
8	b	Desiree	8	e	Medard
9	c	Gregory N[azianzen]	9	f	Felicia
10	d	Gordianus	10	g	Marguerite *R.* [Queen?]
11	e	*Mamer*	11	A	Barnabus
12	f	Nereus	12	b	Jeanne
13	g	John of *S-*	13	c	Anthony of P[adua]
14	A	Pachomius, a[bbot]	14	d	Basil
15	b	*Torquat*	15	e	*Vit, Mod. Cr.*
16	c	*Ubald*	16	f	J[ohn] F[rancis] Regis
17	d	*Pastral*	17	g	Avitus
18	e	Honorius	18	A	Marino
19	f	Yves	19	b	Julianne
20	g	Bernard	20	c	Silverius
21	A	*Hospice.*	21	d	Heloise
22	b	Julie	22	e	Paulin
23	c	Didier	23	f	Audrey
24	d	Vincent of *L.*	24	g	*N. S.* John B[aptist]
25	e	*Donatien*	25	A	Prosper
26	f	Philip of *N.*	26	b	John and Paul
27	f	Jules	27	c	Crescent
28	A	Germain	28	d	Irene
29	b	Maximus	29	e	Peter and Paul
30	c	Felix	30	f	Com[mon] of St. Paul
31	d	Petronilla			

Appendix

JULY			AUGUST		
The Month has 31 *days and the Moon* 30.			*The Month has* 31 *days and the Moon* 30.		
1	g	Martial	1	c	Cyril
2	A	*The Visitation of Our Lady*	2	d	Stephen P[ope]
3	b	Anatole	3	e	Stephanie
4	c	*Tr.* of St. Mart[in?]	4	f	Dominick
5	d	Zoe	5	g	*Emygde*
6	e	*Tranquillin*	6	A	Transfiguration of Our Lord
7	f	Lucien	7	b	*Gaetan* [Galien?]
8	g	Elizabeth	8	c	Syriac
9	A	Zenon	9	d	Roman
10	b	Felicity	10	e	Philomena
11	c	Pelagius	11	f	Suzanne
12	d	*Gualbert*	12	g	Clare
13	e	*Anaclet*	13	A	Hypolite
14	f	Bonaventure	14	b	Eusebius
15	g	Henry	15	c	Assumption
16	A	O[ur] L[ady] of M[t.] Carm[el]	16	d	Hyacinth
17	b	Alexis	17	e	*Mamès*
18	c	Camille of *L.*	18	f	Helen
19	d	Vincent de P[aul]	19	g	Louis, bishop
20	e	Marguerite *V.* [Virgin?]	20	A	Bernard
21	f	*Praxède*	21	b	*Privat*
22	g	Magdalena, Madeleine	22	c	*Symphorien*
23	A	Appolinus	23	d	Philip *Ben.*
24	b	Christine	24	e	Bartholomew
25	c	James	25	f	Louis, king of F[rance]
26	d	Anne	26	g	*Zéphirin*
27	e	*Pantaléon*	27	A	Caesar [bishop]
28	f	*Nazaire*	28	b	Augustine
29	g	Martha	29	c	Death of S[t.] J[ohn the] B[aptist]
30	A	*Abdon* [martyr]	30	d	Rose.—[St.] *Fiac[re]*
31	b	Ignatius L[oyola]	31	e	Raymond

Appendix

		SEPTEMBER			OCTOBER
		The Month has 30 *days* *and the Moon* 29.			*The Month has* 31 *days* *and the Moon* 30.
1	f	Giles	1	A	*Remì*
2	g	*Hermogène*	2	b	Guardian Angels
3	A	St. Simon	3	c	Girard
4	b	Rosalie	4	d	Francis of Assisi
5	c	Laurent	5	e	*Placide*
6	d	Onesiphore	6	f	Bruno
7	e	*Reine*	7	g	Julie
8	f	Nativity of Our Lady	8	A	Brigitt
9	g	Omar [bishop]	9	b	Dennis, bishop
10	A	Nicholas	10	c	Francis Borgia
11	b	Hyacinth	11	d	Necaise
12	c	Sacerdos	12	e	Wilfred
13	d	Aimee	13	f	Edward
14	e	Exaltation of the Holy Cross	14	g	Caliste
15	f	Nicomedius	15	A	Theresa
16	g	Cornelius *(Eup.)*	16	b	Edvige, abbot
17	A	7 D[eath of the] V[irgin] M[ary?]	17	c	*Cerboney*
18	b	Sophie	18	d	Luke
19	c	January	19	e	*Savinien*
20	d	Eustasius	20	f	*Sendon*
21	e	Matthew	21	g	Hilarion
22	f	Maurice	22	A	Melanie
23	g	Tecla	23	b	Severin
24	A	*Andoche*	24	c	*Magloire*
25	b	*Cleophas*	25	d	Crespin
26	c	Justine	26	e	Evariste
27	d	*Côme*	27	f	*Frumen.*
28	e	Wenceslas	28	g	Simon and Jude
29	f	Michael	29	A	Theodore
30	g	Jerome	30	b	*Lucain* [Lucian?]
			31	c	Quentin

		NOVEMBER			DECEMBER
		The Month has 30 *days* *and the Moon* 30.			*The Month has* 31 *days* *and the Moon* 29.
1	d	All Saints	1	f	Eligius
2	e	The Dead	2	g	Bibiana
3	f	Marcel	3	A	Francis Xav[ier]
4	g	Charles	4	b	Barbara
5	A	Bertilda	5	c	*Sabbas*
6	b	Leonard	6	d	Nicholas, bishop
7	c	Engelbert	7	e	Ambrose
8	d	*Dieudonne*	8	f	[Immaculate] Conception
9	e	Mathurin	9	g	Leocadie
10	f	Demetrius	10	A	Eulalie
11	g	Martin, bishop	11	b	*Damase*
12	A	Didier	12	c	Constance
13	b	Brice	13	d	Lucy
14	c	*Maclou*	14	e	Arsene
15	d	Eugene	15	f	Valerian
16	e	Eucher	16	g	Adelaide
17	f	*Agnan*	17	A	Olympiad
18	g	*Odon*	18	b	Gratien
19	A	Elizabeth of H[ungary]	19	c	Timoleon
20	b	Edmund	20	d	Zenon
21	c	Pres[entation] of O[ur] L[ady]	21	e	Thomas, ap[ostle]
22	d	Cecile	22	f	*Ischyrion*
23	e	Clement	23	g	Victoria
24	f	Flora	24	A	Delphine
25	g	Catherine	25	b	Christmas
26	A	*Victorine* [Victoria?]	26	c	Stephen
27	b	*Maxime*	27	d	John, bishop
28	c	Sosthene	28	e	Innocent
29	d	Saturnin	29	f	Thomas *C.*
30	e	Andrew	30	g	*Benyer*
31	A	Silvester			

TRANSLATOR'S NOTES

➤━◆➤━◦━◄◆━◄

1. I.e., with lime.

2. The French nurseryman Louis Claude Noisette defined *terre froid* as soil coming from a northern exposure with too much aluminum, being heavy and compact and poor in transmitting water (Noisette, *Manuel complet du jardinier,* 54).

3. *Scorsonera hispanica.*

4. Lelièvre uses *crouvrez* here but probably means *couvrez,* cover.

5. Lelièvre uses *gombo* here for *okra,* also spelled *gombaud* in France *(Hibiscus esculentus).*

6. *Fraise ananas (Fraisier grandifolia,* wild), a large fruiting variety.

7. Lelièvre may here mean *Mespilus azarolus,* a tree native to southern France.

8. *Mespilus germanica* L., a small, deciduous tree with edible, apple-shaped fruit.

9. There seems to be no direct English equivalent for this word. In the passage, Lelièvre is clearly referring to the practice of disbudding *(ebourgeonnement),* and also to pinching, both of which are features of the *palissage* operation.

10. Probably *Ocymum grandiflorum* L'Herit.

11. *Le Bon Jardinier* (1836, p. 692) mentions that there are sixty-nine varieties of *Cacalia sagittata.*

12. *Le Bon Jardinier* (1836) lists twelve species of *chèvrefeuilles.*

13. *Agrostemma coeli rosa* L. (rose of heaven).

14. The dahlia was introduced into France from Mexico about 1800 and

quickly became one of the top favorites of growers and the focus of many large European flower shows. By Lelièvre's time there were over one hundred named varieties, so mixed that Parisian horticulturists had given up trying to classify them (*Le Bon Jardinier* [1836], 713–17).

15. Lelièvre may be referring to *Dolichos lignosus* L. or *Phaseolus coccineus* L., known in France as *haricot d'espagne*.

16. *Le Bon Jardinier* (1836) lists fourteen species of jasmine.

17. The particular description given here is for the species *hibiscus manihot*, in French *ketmie à feuilles de Manihot*, taken directly from *Le Bon Jardinier*; but Parisian nurserymen were also growing *H. pedunculatus, H. mutabilis, H. abelmoschus, H. rosa sinensis, H. moscheutos, H. militaris, H. Syriacus, H. palustris*, and three other species in hothouses and *orangeries* at this time.

18. *L. pinnata (Le Bon Jardinier)*.

19. *L. elegans (Le Bon Jardinier)*.

20. *Convallaria maialis flore purpurescente Herb. de l'Amateur Vol. 1 (Le Bon Jardinier)*.

21. *C. maialis flore pleno. Herb. de l'Amateur Vol. 1 (Le Bon Jardinier)*.

22. Sixteen are listed in *Le Bon Jardinier*.

23. Trailing vinca *(Vinca major)* is *pervenche grande* in French; the erect vinca *(Vinca minor)* is *pervenche petite*.

24. *Philadelphus* was sometimes called *seringa* or *syringa*, but "*this* name belongs to the lilac" (L. H. Bailey and Ethel Zoe Bailey, comps., *Hortus Second: A Concise Dictionary of Gardening, General Horticulture and Cultivated Plants in North America* [New York: Macmillan, 1949], 555).

25. *Le Bon Jardinier* (1836, p. 770) lists all four of the *thlaspis* (candytufts), including the *julienne*, but does not provide a Latin name for the last one, nor was this name listed in other sources consulted.

26. Lelièvre is probably referring to *Lippia citriodora* (lemon verbena), and four other species, *Verbena aubletia, V. melindres, V. pulchella*, and *V. venosa*, all listed in *Le Bon Jardinier*.

27. This may be *Verbena rigida*, the "wild verbena," or the "sand verbena . . . native to Texas and west Louisiana" (Neil Odenwald and James Turner,

Identification, Selection, and Use of Southern Plants for Landscape Design, 3rd ed. [Baton Rouge: Claitor's Publishing Division, 1996], 612).

28. *Viola odorata* L.

29. *Le Bon Jardinier* lists *Zinnia multiflora,* the yellow-centered red zinnia, as a native of Louisiana.

30. *Rune* is used here, perhaps a typographical error for *une.*

GLOSSARY

Adherent *[Adhérant]*—Strongly attached, as [if] welded.

Annual *[Annuel]*—Said of plants that last only one year.

Axil *[Aisselle]*—Angle formed by a leaf on a branch, a branch on a larger branch, or a branch on the stem, etc.

Axillary *[Axillaire]*—Departing from the axil.

Biennial *[Bisannuel]*—That which lasts two years.

Blind (one-eyed) *[Borgne]*—Without a terminal bud; blind cabbage, that which has no heart and cannot sprout. By cutting its leaves near the trunk, it makes shoots in the leaf axils.

Buds *[Boutons]*—Buds located in the axils of the leaves and at the end[s] of the branches. It is from buds that branches sprout.

Buds *[Bourgeons]*—Leaves and branches beginning to develop.

Bunches *[Grappes]*—Said of flowers arranged like bunches of grapes.

Creeping *[Rampant]*—Lying on the ground.

Crest *[Aigrette]*—Tufts of hair at the top of certain seeds, such as thistle, etc.

Cut back *[Rabattre]*—To cut the branches of a tree back to their joint with the trunk, in order to rejuvenate it.

Disk *[Disque]*—The center of composite flowers; the rays surround the disk.

Double *[Double]*—Flower of which the petals are well multiplied.

Eye *[Oeil]*—Small point which appears on trees and shrubs, in leaf axils, and which form[s], the following spring, wood and fruit buds.

Friable *[Meuble]*—Said of earth well broken and without clumps.

Genus *[Genre]*—Union of species which have common relationships according to their botanical characteristics.

Germination *[Germination]*—The moment when the swollen seed opens to develop the plant that it contains.

Hair roots *[Chevelu]*—Roots as fine as hairs; it is these that take in nourishing juices to transmit them to the larger roots, from which they pass into the stem, etc.

Hands or tendrils *[Mains* or *vrilles]*—Threads by means of which certain plants attach themselves to surrounding features.

Hardy *[Rustique]*—Not difficult to grow; accommodating to all soils, and to all exposures.

Head (crown) *[Tête]*—A group of branches extending in every direction above the trunk; round and globular flowers.

Herbaceous *[Herbacé]*—Said of plants and of green, soft, and succulent stems.

Hoeing *[Binage]*—Light plowing, given after planting.

Ligneous *[Ligneux]*—That which is of the nature of wood.

Neck *[Collet]*—A kind of node which is found between the root and the stem.

Perennial *[Vivace]*—That which lasts several years.

Petals *[Pétales]*—Leaves, ordinarily colored, of which the flower is composed. They are also called floral leaves.

Petiole *[Pétiole]*—This is the stem of the leaf.

Pinch *[Pincer]*—To cut with the fingers the part of the plant that one wants to shorten.

Plant *[Plante]*—Name common to all vegetation.

Pollen *[Pollen]*—The fertile powder of plants.

Rambling *[Sarmenteux]*—Of which the stems are long and flexible like those of a vine.

Rays *[Rayons]*—Petals surrounding the disk, and arranged in rays.

Run, running *[Tracer, traçant]*—Said of roots that spread across two beds *[terres]* and make sprouts.

Semidouble *[Semi-double]*—That which has more petals than a simple flower, and fewer than a double.

Sensitivity *[Irritabilité]*—Kind of responsiveness in certain plants when they are touched.

Sever *[Sevrer]*—To cut and separate from the mother plant layers which have taken root.

Shelving bed *[Ados]*—A sloping ground is so called; I have used this word to designate an artificial wall, a[30] fence that serves to shelter the plants set against it.

Single *[Simple]*—Flower having a simple range of petals, some more elaborate than others. These are the most likely to have seeds.

Solitaire *[Solitaire]*—Isolated, single.

Spur *[Eperon]*—A kind of point opposite the petals in certain flowers. [Nasturtium, violet.]

Stake *[Tuteur]*—Support given to stems that are too weak to support themselves alone, or to straighten out those that are not straight.

Starry (enfeebled) *[Etoilé]*—Said of plants which, deprived of air or light, have no substance. Sown too thickly, plants become enfeebled.

Stem *[Tige]*—This is the part of the plant that is connected to the root, and from which the branches grow.

Stock *[Sujet]*—This is the tree that is destined to be grafted [upon].

Taproot *[Pivot]*—Large root that is buried perpendicularly in the earth.

Terminal *[Terminal]*—That which is found at the end of boughs or branches.

Thorn *[Epine]*—Hard, needle-shaped point attached to wood, which cannot be removed without wounding the plant.

Thorns *[Aiguillons]*—Pricks found along the bark that can be detached without wounding it, as with roses.

Twig *[Brindille]*—Thin and short fruit branch. Also called a *lambourde.*

Umbel *[Ombelle]*—Flower [head] shaped like an umbrella.

Variegated *[Panaché]*—Of various colors.

Weed (verb) *[Sarcler]*—This is to remove weeds, either by hand, or with the assistance of a tool called a weeder or scraper.

Whorled *[Verticillé]*—Leaves, flowers or branches arranged in a ring around the stem.

Wild *[Sauvageon]*—Tree that has not been grafted or that sprouts in the woods. Those produced from seed, from which the fruit is cultured, are called *free.*

BIBLIOGRAPHY

➤—┤◆├—○—┤◆├—◄

Published and Secondary Works

Allain, Mathé. *Not Worth a Straw: French Colonial Policy and the Early Years of Louisiana.* Lafayette, La.: Center for Louisiana Studies, University of Southwestern Louisiana, 1988.

Bailey, L. H., and Ethel Zoe Bailey, comps. *Hortus Second: A Concise Dictionary of Gardening, General Horticulture and Cultivated Plants in North America.* New York: Macmillan, 1949.

Barnhill, Georgia Brady, Diana Korzenik, and Caroline F. Sloat, eds. *The Cultivation of Artists in Nineteenth-Century America.* Worcester, Mass.: American Antiquarian Society, 1997.

Becker, Robert F. "Gardening for Profit: Supplying America's Cities with Vegetables Prior to 1900." In *Proceedings of the 1990 Annual Meeting,* Association for Living Historical Farms and Agricultural Museums.

Brasseaux, Carl A. *The Foreign French: Nineteenth-Century French Immigration to Louisiana.* Vol. 1, *1820–1839.* Lafayette, La.: Center for Louisiana Studies, University of Southwestern Louisiana, 1990.

Bullion, Brenda. "Early American Farming and Gardening Literature: 'Adapted to the Climates and Seasons of the United States.'" *Journal of Garden History* 12, no. 1 (1992): 29–51.

Buist, Robert. *American Flower-Garden Directory: Containing Practical Directions for the Culture of Plants in the Flower Garden, Hot-House, Green-House, Rooms, or Parlor Windows, For Every Month in the Year.*

With A Description of the Plants Most Desirable in Each, the Nature of the Soil, and Situation Best Adapted to their Growth, The Proper Season for Transplanting, etc. With Instructions for Erecting A Hot-House, Green-House, and Laying Out a Flower Garden. The Whole Adapted to Either Large or Small Gardens. With Instructions for Preparing the Soil, Propagating, Planting, Pruning, Training and Fruiting the Grapevine. With Descriptions of the Best Sorts For Cultivating in the Open Air. Fourth Edition, with Numerous Additions. By Robert Buist, Nurseryman and Seed Grower. Philadelphia: A. Hart, 1851.

Castellanos, Henry C. *New Orleans As it Was: Episodes of Louisiana Life.* 1895. Reprint, Baton Rouge: Louisiana State University Press, 1978.

Davy de Virville, Ad. *Histoire de la botanique en France.* Paris, 1954.

Dezanche, Mons. *Précis Elémentaire de Géographie à L'Usage des Ecoles Américaines.* New Orleans: J. F. Lelièvre, 1841.

Duval, Marguerite. *The King's Garden.* Trans. Annette Tomarken and Claudine Cowen. Charlottesville: University Press of Virginia, 1982.

Fessender, Thomas G. *The New American Gardener, Containing Practical Directions on the Culture of Fruits and Vegetables including Landscape and Ornamental Gardening, Grape-vines, Silk, Strawberries, Etc. by Thomas G. Fessender, Editor of The New England Farmer.* Boston: J. B. Russell, 1828.

Furman, James L. *Reminiscences of an Octogenarian or the Autobiography of a School Teacher.* New Orleans: Office Baptist Visitor, 1904.

Goudeau, John M. "Booksellers and Printers in New Orleans, 1764–1885." *Journal of Library History* 5, no. 1 (1970).

Institute de France, Section d'Agriculture. *Nouveau cours complet d'agriculture théorique et practique, contenant la grande et la petite culture, l'économie rurale et domestique, la médecine vétérinaire, etc.; ou, Dictionnaire raisonnée et universel d'agriculture; ouvrage rédigé sur le plan de celui de feu l'abbé Rozier, duquel on a conservé les articles dont la bonté a été prouvée par l'expérience; par les membres de la Section d'a-*

griculture de l'Institut de France, etc. Nouvelle ed., revue, corrigée et augmenteé. Paris: à la librairie encyclopédique de Roret, *ca.* 1821–23.

Jumonville, Florence M. "Books, Libraries, and Undersides for the Skies of Beds: The Extraordinary Career of A. L. Boimare." *Louisiana History* 34, no. 4 (1993): 437–59.

Leiris, Mme. *L'Histoire des Etats-Unis, Racontée aux Enfans.* Paris, 1835. Reprint, New Orleans: J. F. Lelièvre, 1845.

Lelièvre, J. F. *Nouveau Jardinier de la Louisiane.* New Orleans: J. F. Lelièvre, 1838.

Lemoine, Pierre. *Versailles in Color.* Versailles, 1981.

"Le Jardin des Plantes D'Hier a Aujourd'hui." Liberté de Normandie (Caen), 1976.

Liger, Louis. *Le Jardinier Fleuriste; ou, la Culture Universele des Fleurs, Arbres, Arbustes.* Paris, 1787.

Lussan, Auguste. *La Famille Creole, drame en cinq actes et en prose.* New Orleans: Chez Fremaux et Alfted Moret, 1837.

du Monceau, Henri-Louis Duhamel. *Traité des arbres fruitiers contenant leur figure, leur descriptions. . . .* Paris, 1768.

Noisette, M. Louis. *Manuel Complet du Jardinier, Marâicher, Pépinièriste, Botaniste, Fleuriste, et Paysagiste.* 4 vols. Paris: Audot, 1826.

———. *Manuel Complet du Jardinier . . . .* Brussels, 1829.

Odenwald, Neil, and James Turner. *Identification Selection and Use of Southern Plants for Landscape Design.* 3rd ed. Baton Rouge: Claitor's Publishing Division, 1996.

Oxford University Press. *Oxford Superlex: The Oxford Hachette Dictionary English-French.* Compact Disk, Ver. 1.1. Oxford, 1994–96.

Patrick, Walter R., and Cecil G. Taylor, "A Louisiana French Plantation Library, 1842." *The French-American Review* (January–March, 1948): 47–67.

Pitts and Clark. *City Directory for New Orleans.* New Orleans, 1842.

Rafinesque, Constantine Samuel. *Florula ludoviciana; or, A flora of the* state of Louisiana. *Tr., rev., and improved from the French of C. C. Robin, by C. S. Rafinesque.* New York: C. Wiley, 1817.

Robinson, W. *Gleanings from French Gardens, Comprising an Account of Such Features of French Horticulture as Are most Worthy of Adoption in British Gardens.* 2nd ed. London: Frederick Warne, 1869.

Rozier, Abbé François. *Cours Complet d'Agriculture, théorique, practique, économique, et de médecine rurale et veterinaire: suivi d'une méthode pour étudier l'agriculture par principes; ou, Dictionnaire universel d'agriculture/par un société d'agriculteurs, et redigé par M. L'Abbé Rozier.* 12 vols. Paris/Lyons: Chez les Libraires associés, 1793–1805.

Sauder, Robert A. "The Origin and Spread of the Public Market System in New Orleans," *Louisiana History* 22, no. 3 (1981): 281–97.

Sedella, Père Antoine de. *Abregé du Catéchisme de la Louisiane . . . Nouvelle ed., Approuvé. Par le Très Reverend Père Antoine de Sedella, Curé de l'église paroissale de la Nouvelle Orléans.* New Orleans: 1818.

Smith, Thomas. *French Gardening.* London, 1909.

Société de Naturalistes et d'Agriculteurs. *Dictionnaire d'Histoire Naturelle, Appliqué aux Arts, Principalement à l'Agriculture et à l'économie rurale et domestique: Par une Societé de Naturalistes et d'Agriculteurs.* 23 vols. Nouvelle ed. Paris: Deterville, 1803.

Turner, Suzanne. "Roots of a Regional Garden Tradition: The Drawings of the New Orleans Notarial Archives." In *Regional Garden Design in the United States.* Ed. Therese O'Malley and Marc Treib. Washington, D.C.: Dumbarton Oaks Research Library and Collection, 1995.

———, and A. J. Meek. *The Gardens of Louisiana.* Baton Rouge: Louisiana State University Press, 1997.

Vicknair, Ulger. *Le Jardinier Economique et Productif.* New Orleans, 1867.

Weathers, John. *French Market-Gardening, Including Practical Details of "Intensive Cultivation" for English Growers.* London, 1909.

Bibliography

Work Projects Administration of Louisiana, Survey of Federal Archives in Louisiana. *Passenger Lists Taken from Manifests of the Customs Service in New Orleans.* Ed. Stanley C. Arthur. Vol. 2, *1834–1838.* New Orleans, 1940.

Manuscript and Primary Materials

From the Historic New Orleans Collection

d'Estréhan, Nicholas Noel. Papers. Diary.
Vieux Carré Survey.

From the New Orleans Public Library, Louisiana Division

L'Abeille. January 26, 1842.
Charles Jourdan v A. L. Boimare. 1JDC 6079.
Le Courrier de la Louisiane. October 12, 1830.
Succession of Charles Jourdan. Court of Probates for the Parish of Orleans, 1834. Microfilm roll 116.
Succession of J. F. Lelièvre. 2DC 7441. Microfilm VSB290/7398–7531.

From the Tulane University Howard-Tilton Memorial Library Special Collections

Almanach de J. F. Lelièvre/Calculé Pour La Nouvelle-Orléans Pour L'Année 1871, et Après le 4 Juillet La 98.e de L'Independance Américaine. New Orleans, 1871.
Caillé Lelièvre letters. MS B58.
De Feriet Letter Books.

From the New Orleans Notarial Archives

Acts of R. Brenan, Notary Public (hereafter N.P.), 1853.
Acts of H. B. Cenas, N.P., 1834.

Acts of F. D. Charbonnet, N.P., 1925.

Acts of Joseph Cuvillier, N.P., 1847.

Acts of Michel de Armas, N.P., 1819.

Acts of Octave de Armas, N.P., 1832.

Acts of A. Dreyfous, N.P., 1846.

Acts of Amedée Ducatel, N.P., 1854.

Acts of L. Feraud, N.P., 1836.

Acts of Theodore Guyol, N.P., 1872.

Acts of Hugues Lavergne, N.P., 1823.

Acts of A. Mazureau, N.P., 1842.

Acts of J. F. Meunier, N.P., 1880, 1894.

Acts of Hughes Pedesclaux, N.P., 1834.

Acts of W. H. Peters, N.P., 1855.

Acts of Carlile Pollock, N.P., 1835, 1838.

Acts of Jacob Soria, N.P., 1851.

Acts of Sol Weiss, N.P., 1926.

"Plan d'une Propriété Dans le 3.M Municipalité," Plan Book 21, [Jacques] dePouilly, May 8, 1847.

INDEX

➤━┥━◆➤━○━◆┝━◅

Index

Index

Index

J.-F. LELIÈVRE, 174, rue

ET A LA SUCCURSALE, RUE

LIBRAIRIE CL

Française, Anglais

ARTICLES DE PIÉTÉ

...lets monture or, argent et acier. — Étuis
...apelets en or, ivoire, émail et coco. —
...a de toutes sortes or et argent. — Statuettes
...s grandeur pour Oratoires. — Médaillons
...argent. — Reliquaires en or et argent. —
...Crucifix portatifs en or et argent, Ivoire,
...bène, Jaspe et Cornaline, etc. — Tableaux
..., Sujets sacrés. — Imagerie très-fine pour
...e prières. — Gravures encadrées et non
...s. — Livrés de prières, Reliures, Ivoire,
...caille, Velours, Moire et Chagrin garnis en
...t et aluminium. — Prie-Dieu pour Ora-
...hapelle.

ORNE

Chasubles, Dalmatiques, Chapes et Étoles pastorales selon le Rit
Voiles de bénédiction. — Aubes et Cordons d'Aubes. — Calices, C
Ostensoirs, Burettes en or, argent et vermeil. — Croix de proc
Bénitiers, Encensoirs dorés et argentés. — Chandeliers d'autel d
argentés, avec leur souches. — Cierges pour autel et pour pr
communion de toutes dimensions en cire très-pure.

Maison de Commission à

	JUILLET ♌			AOUT ♏			SEPTEMBRE ♎	
	le soleil entre au Lion le 22.			*Le soleil entre au Scorpion le 22.*			*Le soleil entre à la Balance le*	
	le 6, à 11 h. 42 m. matin.		D. Q. le 4, à 4 h. 27 m. soir.			D. Q. le 2, à 10 h. 35 m. s		
	Ondées fréquentes.		Beau.			Beau.		
	le 13, à 10 h. 9 m. matin		N. L. le 11, à 9 h. 40 m. soir.			N. L. le 10, à 11 h. 51 m.		
	Ondées fréquentes.		Beau par nord, pluie par sud.			Ondées fréquentes.		
	le 21, à 7 h. 12 m. matin.		P. Q. le 20, à 0 h. 34 m. matin.			P. Q. le 18, à 4 h. 46 m. so		
	Pluie et vent.		Beau.			Beau.		
	le 28, à 10 h. 23 m. soir.		P. L. le 27, à 7 h. 9 m. matin.			P. L. le 25, à 3 h. 47 m. s		
	Beau.		Pluie.			Variable.		

Mercredi.	Martial.	1	Samedi.	Cyrille.	1	Mardi.	Leu et Gilles.
eudi.	Visit. de Notre-Dame.	2	**Dim.**	Étienne, pape et mar.	2	Mercredi.	Hermogène.
'endredi.	Anatole.	3	Lundi.	Stéphanie.	3	Jeudi.	Siméon Stylit
Samedi.	*Anniv. de l'Indépend.*	4	Mardi.	Dominique.	4	Vendredi.	Rosalie.
Dim.	Zoé.	5	Mercredi.	Emygde, év. et mart.	5	Samedi.	Laurent Justi
undi.	Tranquillin.	6	Jeudi.	Tr. de N.-S.	6	**Dim.**	Onésyphore.
Mardi.	Lucien.	7	Vendredi.	Gaétan.	7	Lundi.	Reine.
Mercredi.	Elisabeth, reine du P.	8	Samedi.	Cyriaque.	8	Mardi.	Nat. de N.-D.
eudi.	Zenon.	9	**Dim.**	Romain, év.	9	Mercredi.	Omer.
'endredi.	Félicité.	10	Lundi.	Laurent, martyr.	10	Jeudi.	Nicolas.
Samedi.	Pélagie.	11	Mardi.	Philomène. Suzanne.	11	Vendredi.	Hyacinthe.
Dim.	Jean Gualbert.	12	Mercredi.	Claire.	12	Samedi.	Sacerdos.
undi.	Anaclet.	13	Jeudi.	Hippolyte.	13	**Dim.**	Aimé.
Mardi.	Bonaventure.	14	Vendredi.	Eusèbe. *V.-Jeûne.*	14	Lundi.	Exaltation S
Mercredi.	Henri, empereur.	15	Samedi.	Assomption.	15	Mardi.	Nicomède.
eudi.	N. D. du Mont-Carmel	16	**Dim.**	Hyacinthe.	16	Mercredi.	*IV Temps.* (
'endredi.	Alexis.	17	Lundi.	Mamès.	17	Jeudi.	François.
Samedi.	Camille de Lellis.	18	Mardi.	Hélène.	18	Vendredi.	Sophie.
Dim.	Vincent de Paul.	19	Mercredi.	Louis, évêque.	19	Samedi.	Janvier.
undi.	Marguerite.	20	Jeudi.	Bernard.	20	**Dim.**	Eustache.
Mardi.	Praxède.	21	Vendredi.	Privat.	21	Lundi.	Mathieu.
Mercredi.	Madeleine.	22	Samedi.	Symphorien.	22	Mardi.	Maurice.
eudi.	Apollinaire de Rav.	23	**Dim.**	Philippe Béniti.	23	Mercredi.	Thècle.
'endredi.	Christine. *Jourscanic.*	24	Lundi.	Barthélemi.	24	Jeudi.	Andoche.
Samedi.	Jacques le Mineur.	25	Mardi.	Louis, roi.	25	Vendredi.	Cléophas.
Dim.	Anne.	26	Mercredi.	Zéphirin. *Fin des J.C.*	26	Samedi.	Justine.
undi.	Pantaléon.	27	Jeudi.	Césaire d'Arles.	27	**Dim.**	Côme.
Mardi.	Nazaire.	28	Vendredi.	Augustin.	28	Lundi.	Wenceslas.
Mercredi.	Marthe.	29	Samedi.	Décol. de s. Jean-B.	29	Mardi.	Michel, ar.
eudi.	Abdon.	30	**Dim.**	Rose. Fiacre.	30	Mercredi.	Jérôme.
endredi.	Ignace de Loyola.	31	Lundi.	Raymond.			

	LEVER DU SOLEIL		COUCHER DU SOLEIL	
	Temps moyen de la Nouvelle-Orléans.	MOIS	Temps moyen de la Nouvelle-Orléan
...	Le 1 à 5h03s, le 7 à 5h07s, le 15 à 5h12s, le 22 à 5h14s	Juillet...	Le 1 à 7h03s, le 7 à 7h03s, le 15 à 7h »s, le 2
...	...à 5 20, le 7 à 5 23, le 15 à 5 27, le 22 à 5 30	Août...	Le 1 à 7 06, le 7 à 7 »s, le 15 à 6